QUEER EDWARD II
by
Derek Jarman

BFI Publishing

First published in 1991 by the
British Film Institute
21 Stephen Street
London W1P 1PL

Reprinted 1992

British Library Cataloguing in Publication Data
Jarman, Derek
  Queer, Edward II
  1. Title
  791.4372

  ISBN 0-85170-316-x

Design and typesetting by Translations
31 Councillor Street
London SE5 0LY

Printed in Great Britain by
The Trinity Press, Worcester

QUEER EDWARD II

How to make a film of a gay love affair and get it commissioned.
Find a dusty old play and violate it.

It is difficult enough to be queer, but to be a queer in the cinema is
almost impossible. Heterosexuals have fucked up the screen so
completely that there's hardly room for us to kiss there. Marlowe
outs the past - why don't we out the present? That's really the only
message this play has. Fuck poetry. The best lines in Marlowe
sound like pop songs and the worst, well, we've tried to spare you
them...

This book is dedicated to:
the repeal of all anti-gay laws, particularly
Section 28

THE FILM

Cast in order of appearance			
Edward II	*Steven Waddington*	Sexy Girls	*Liz Ranken*
Lightborn	*Kevin Collins*		*Renee Eyre*
Gaveston	*Andrew Tiernan*		*Sharon Munro*
Spencer	*John Lynch*		*Daniel Bevan*
Bishop of Winchester	*Dudley Sutton*	Youths	*Ian Francis*
Isabella	*Tilda Swinton*		*James Norton*
Kent	*Jerome Flynn*		*Tristam Cones*
Prince Edward	*Jody Graber*	Elektra Quartet	*Jocelyn Pook (Viola)*
Mortimer	*Nigel Terry*		*Abigail Brown (Violin)*
Chorus of Nobility	*Jill Balcon*		*Sonia Slany (Violin)*
	Barbara New		*Dinah Beamish (Cello)*
	Andrea Miller		
	Brian Mitchell	'Edward II'	*the film*
	David Glover	based on the play by	*Christopher Marlowe*
	John Quentin		*A Working Title Production*
	Andrew Charleston		
Bishop	*Roger Hammond*	Exectuive Producers	*Sarah Radclyffe*
Poet	*Allan Corduner*		*Simon Curtis*
Singer	*Annie Lennox*	Executive Producer (Japan)	*Takashi Asai*
Captive Policeman	*Tony Forsyth*		
Dancers	*Lloyd Newson*	Associate Director	*Ken Butler*
	Nigel Charnock	Camera Operator	*Ian Wilson*
Sailors	*Mark Davis*	Sound Recordist	*George Richards*
	Andy Jeffrey	Art Director	*Rick Eyres*
Man with Snake	*Barry John Clarke*		
Altar Boys	*John Henry Duncan*	1st Assistant Director	*Cilla Ware*
	Thomas Duncan	Script Supervisor	*Pearl Morrison*
Soldiers on Guard	*Giles de Montigny*	Production Manager	*Sarah Swords*
	Jonathon Stables	Production Designer	*Christopher Hobbs*
	Michael Watkins	Music	*Simon Fisher-Turner*
	Robb Dennis		
	David Oliver	Editor	*George Akers*
	Chris McHallem	Photography	*Ian Wilson*
	Chris Adamson	Screenplay	*Derek Jarman*
	Danny Earl		*Stephen McBride*
Wild Girls	*Kim Dare*		*Ken Butler*
	Kristina Overton		
Gym Instructor	*Trevor Skingle*	Producers	*Steve Clark-Hall*
Equery	*Christopher Hobbs*		*Antony Root*
Seamstresses	*Sandy Powell*		
	Kate Temple		
Masseur	*Andrew Lee Bolton*	Directed by	*Derek Jarman*

THE FILM CREW

Production Coordinator	*Mairi Bett*	Electricians	*Dave Brown*
2nd Asssistant Director	*Ian Francis*		*Steven Read*
3rd Assistant Director	*Jeremy Johns*		*Colin Powton*
Floor Runners	*Daniel Bevan*		
	James Norton	Choreography	*Lloyd Newson*
Production Runners	*Jason Goode*		*Nigel Charnock*
	Julian Woolford	Fight Director	*Malcolm Ranson*
Accountant	*Rachel James*	Assistant Fight Director	*Nicholas Hall*
Accounts Assistant	*Debbie Moore*	Additional Casting	*Ian Francis*
		Crowd Casting	*Lee's People*
Focus Puller	*Kenny Byrne*		
Clapper Loader	*Ros Naylor*	Construction Manager	*Steve Ede*
Grip	*Malcolm Huse*	S/B Stagehand	*Derek Ede*
Camera Dept Trainee	*Tristam Cones*	S/B Carpenter	*David Lee*
		S/B Rigger	*Dave Tubbs*
Stills Photographer	*Liam Longman*	S/B Painter	*William Lowe*
		Rigger	*Nigel Crafts*
Dubbing mixer	*Peter Maxwell*	Carpenter	*James Muir*
Assistant Dubbing Mixer	*Mick Boggis*		
Sound Recordist	*Bill McCarthy*	Music Performed by	*Simon Fisher Turner*
Boom Operator	*Pete Murphy*		*Dean Brodrick*
Sound Jobfit Trainee	*Andrew Griffiths*		*Richard Preston*
			Melanie Peppenheim
Assistant Editor	*Laura Evans*		*Glen Fox*
2nd Assistant Editor	*Hermione Byrt*		
Dubbing Editor	*Ean Wood*	Recorded & Mixed at	*Shrubland Studios*
Assistant Dubbing Editor	*Mike Crowley*		*London*
Editing Jobfit Trainee	*Jake Martin*		*Elephant Studios,*
			Wapping
Wardrobe Supervisor	*Paul Minter*	*Using "Fisher Prestonics"* ©	
Wardrobe Standby	*Clare Spragge*		
Wardrobe Runner	*Kate Temple*	Engineer	*Richard Preston*
Make-up Assistant	*Miri Ben-Shlomo*	Sound Re-Recorded at	*De Lane Lea,*
			London
Prop Master	*David Balfour*	Titles by	*Peter Watson Associates*
Standby Props	*Pat Harkins*		
Art Dept Assistant	*Chris Roope*	Distributed by	*The Sales Co.*
Gaffer	*Norman Smith*		
Best Boy	*Peter Lamb*		

Derek Jarman *(D)*
Ken Butler (Ghost Director) *(G)*
Isabella Regina *(IR)*

OutRage, *the* Gay Activist Group.
London Lesbian & Gay Centre,
67-69 Cowcross Street. EC1
Tel: 071 490 7153.

Written by	*Derek Jarman*	
	Stephen McBride	
	Ken Butler	
	Tilda Swinton	
Edited by	*Keith Collins*	
	Malcolm Sutherland	
Slogans by	*Greg Taylor*	
Slogan Design by	*Derek Westwood*	
Photographs by	*Liam Longman*	
Photos for pp 21,		
47, 93, 105, 149	*Jacqueline Lucas-Palmer*	
Designed by	*Malcolm Sutherland*	
Thanks to	*Agfa UK and Paresh Patel*	
	Marcia Mihotich	
	Louise Stuart-Muir at Computers Unlimited	

Photos behind the camera
The majority of people below worked on the film without appearing in it.

Seq. 6, DV8. *Seq. 8*, Cilla Ware, Ken Butler, Man with Snake, Jody Graber, Derek Jarman. *Seq. 13*, Morag Ross, Steve Waddington. *Seq. 21*, Derek, Ian Wilson. *Seq. 22*, Dudley Sutton, Miri Ben-Shlomo. *Seq. 25*, George Richards. *Seq. 27*, Cilla Ware. *Seq. 29*, Christopher Hobbs. *Seq. 31*, Annie Lennox, Derek Jarman. *Seq. 42*, Sandy Powell. *Seq. 43*, Steve Clarke-Hall, String Quartet. *Seq. 44*, Ken Butler. *Seq. 45 (cont.)*, Steve McBride. *Seq. 51*, Tristam Cones, Ian Francis. *Seq. 53*, Sandy Powell, Paul Minter, Andrew Tiernan, Clare Spragg. *Seq. 56*, Pete Murphy. *Seq. 58*, Simon Turner. *Seq. 70*, Kevin Collins, Sandy Powell. *Seq. 71*, Dave Tubbs, Davey Balfour. *Seq. 75*, Cast & Crew. *Seq. 81*, Morag Ross & Jody Graber.

"When I say silence I mean silence - absolute and complete silence."

Cilla.

On the Set

The LOVE *that* DARES *not* SPEAK ITS name

SEQUENCE 1.

INTERIOR. THE DEATH OF EDWARD I. NIGHT.
EDWARD I, PRINCE EDWARD.

Edward I, in gilded armour, supported by crutches, crashes around a room. He is having a heart attack. His grandson, the future Edward III, looks on holding a torch that casts eerie shadows.

EDWARD I   Edward, Edward.

Blood oozes through the King's vizor.
We hear the sound of a bagpipe lament.

Straight Edward I, Longshanks, the father, obstinate and very cruel. At sixteen he cheerfully cut the nose and ears from an innocent passer-by for sport.

As we shall see, his charming son gets all the blame, and by many historians isn't even allowed his sexuality.

Queer Edward II.

Edward I died on 7 July 1307. His account books list many exotic medicines prescribed for his ill health: a cordial made from amber, jacynth, musk, pearls and gold.

My chemical life splutters on. Each morning I swallow, with increasing difficulty: a cordial of Ritafer, Fansidar, AZT, Pirodoxin, one Calcium Folinate (to counteract the Ritafer) and two Carbamazapepine to stop any fits my damaged brain might bring!

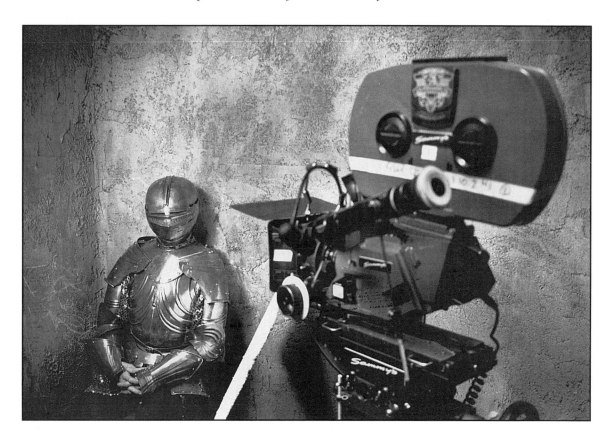

The LOVE *that* CAN'T *keep* ITS BIG MOUTH *shut*

SEQUENCE 2.

INTERIOR. DUNGEON. NIGHT.
EDWARD, LIGHTBORN.

The dungeon is set deep in the earth; a sombre coal cellar. A stagnant pool, the surface of which gleams like beaten lead. Near the edge of the pool, set in the rock, fire issues from the furnace doors.

The foundryman, Lightborn, Edward's jailor, is in his early twenties, his body and hands shaped and coarsened by hard work. His arms and shoulders bare. He is black with coal dust. He is staring at Edward. Sweat forms on his forehead. Edward lies asleep on the floor. Motionless, gaunt. His hands are crossed as if in prayer, crumpled between his fingers is a postcard of London. Lightborn prises this gently from his grasp.

LIGHTBORN (Voice-over - reading the postcard)
My father is deceased; come, Gaveston.

Lightborn folds the postcard into a square. Edward wakes, takes it and recites from memory.

EDWARD My father is deceased; come Gaveston,
And share the Kingdom with thy dearest friend

After 10 weeks of preproduction in Camden we start the shoot at Bray - home of Hammer Horror.

The dungeon resembles the bowels of a hulk, the beached ship of state.

Less is more, says Christopher the designer. No props, except your lamp from Dungeness beach, and a postcard of Piccadilly's Eros. We couldn't find a postcard so Liam, the photographer, took one.

Costume: Edward's duffle coat, monastic CND dropout.

We begin to run the sequence at 8:30 - we finish at 5:30.

ARE *YOU* A CLOSET BIGOT?

SEQUENCE 3.

INTERIOR. BEDROOM. FRANCE. EARLY MORNING.
GAVESTON, 2 HUSTLERS.

The room, with its sand floor, is unfurnished except for a bed.
The two hustlers in bed, naked. Spencer sits on the edge of the
bed.
Gaveston, in a white robe, enters and reads Edward's letter.

GAVESTON   Ah, words that make me surfeit with delight;
               What greater bliss can hap to Gaveston
               Than live and be the favourite of a King?
               (Spencer dresses)

GAVESTON   Sweet prince I come; these, these thy amorous lines
               Might have enforced me to have swum from France,
               And like Leander gasped upon the sand,
               So thou would'st take me in thy arms.
               The sight of London to my exiled eyes
               Is as Elysium to a new come soul;
               Not that I love the city or the men
               But that it harbours him I hold so dear.

Mark and Andy fuck without a blush. Mark said 'What if I get a hard-on?' 'Hide it from the BBC.' The electricians nearly fell out of the lighting grid.

Morocco on the soundtrack. Sex tourism? Young love? True love?

Gaveston's father was a trusted Gascon knight in the service of Edward I. His son was selected as a playmate for the young prince. He was a year older than Edward. Their romance started young, Edward was fifteen.

I searched all year for a book on Piers Gaveston, and found nothing, a great silence.

It is strange that Edward did not disapprove of his son's nature. It was only later when he found that Gaveston had been offered the County of Poitou as a present that all hell broke loose. The loss of land was infinitely more painful than the loss of his son's virginity. Gaveston was banished in a scene. Edward tearing his son's hair out in handfuls. The King went back to his jade chess set.

YOUR CLOSET

Marlowe maintained that those who did not love either boys or tobacco were dead to the world.

SEQUENCE 4.

INTERIOR. BARN. SUNDOWN.
EDWARD, GAVESTON.

The King, stripped to the waist, and Gaveston, naked; lie in each other's arms on straw that cascades from the corner of the room.

GAVESTON   The King, upon whose bosom let me die
(V/O)   And with the world be still at enmity.
           What need the Arctic people love starlight
           To whom the sun shines both by day and night.

YOUR COFFIN

I never had a teenage romance like Edward and Gaveston; the clamped and censorious boarding school stopped any love flowering in its ill-tempered confine.

IT'S IN TO BE OUT

SEQUENCE 5.

INTERIOR. BEDROOM. FRANCE. EARLY MORNING.
GAVESTON, 2 HUSTLERS.

Gaveston by bed. The 2 men in bed. Spencer sitting on the edge of the bed.

GAVESTON (shouts)
Farewell base stooping to the lordly peers;
My knee shall bow to none but to the King.

GAVESTON (aside)
As for the multitude, that are but sparks
Raked up in embers of their poverty.
Fuck them!

GAVESTON (aside)
I'll flatter these and make them live in hope.

GAVESTON
What art thou?

FIRST MAN
A traveller.

GAVESTON
Let me see - thou wouldst do well
To wait at my table,
And tell me lies at dinner time.
And what art thou?

SECOND MAN
A soldier.

GAVESTON
There are hospitals for men like you
I have no war, and therefore sir, begon.

(Gaveston takes a wad of money and passes it to the boys.)

These are not men for me;
I must have wanton poets, pleasant wits,
Musicians that with touching of a string
May draw the pliant King which way I please.

I have to work in the closet. Depending on where you see the film you may or may not see the same cruel cut.

I allowed Channel 4 to cut the hard-on out of 'Sebastian' so that the film could be shown. Should I have done that? Comments on a postcard.

How much information is put out by 'Out On Tuesday' (the gay series on television)? The only thing they have asked me to do was ten minutes on Opera Queens. It is strange how people think of you. Who am I?

My real ambition is to film an act of sodomy (although it would be much more fun to be in it)... But I found out early on that I'm a bad actor. Shame.

HETEROSEXUALITY

SEQUENCE 6.

INTERIOR. THRONE ROOM. NIGHT.
EDWARD, GAVESTON, DANCERS: (DV8).

The room is filled with music. Dancers perform before the King.
Edward sits on his throne in old work clothes, Gaveston has fallen
asleep on his lap.

GAVESTON   Music and poetry is his delight,
(V/O)   Therefore I'll have Italian masques by night
            Sweet speeches, comedies and pleasing shows,
            And in the day, when he shall walk abroad,
            Like Sylvan nymphs my pages shall be clad,
            My men like satyrs grazing on the lawns
            Shall with their goat-feet dance an antic hay.

*It was such a relief when Lloyd
and Nigel of DV8 accepted - I had
been on tenterhooks for weeks.
Then Lloyd fell ill - no wonder
after a breakfast at Bray. I'm on
antibiotics to beat the microwaved
food; he recovered later in the
morning.*

*I ordered the floor to be sand, and
all we could afford was mud.
Lloyd and Nigel danced in a dust-
bath like fighting cocks.*

The dust got everywhere.

*Picture the sad figure of Andreas,
with a watering can, traversing
the set at 8:00 each morning to
damp it down.*

It's a common COMPLAINT

HOMOSEXUALITY

INTERIOR. DUNGEON. NIGHT.
EDWARD, LIGHTBORN.

The King watches Lightborn, undress and wash by the pool.

GAVESTON   Sometime a lovely boy in Dian's shape,
(Distant V/O)   With hair that gilds the water as it glides,
              Crownets of pearl about his naked arms,
              And in his sportful hands an olive tree
              To hide those parts which men delight to see,
              Shall bathe him in a spring, and there hard by
              One like Actaeon peeping through the grove
              Shall by the angry goddess be transformed
              And running in the likeness of an hart,
              By yelping hounds pulled down and seem to die;
              Such things as these best please his majesty.

Marlowe drops classical references like confetti through the text to prove he's up-to-the-minute. Such an intellectual queen.

It's a rare CURE

how
do we terrify?

SEQUENCE 8.

INTERIOR. EMPTY ROOM. TWILIGHT.
PRINCE EDWARD. MAN WITH SNAKE.

The room is deserted, except for a man wearing a crown of golden leaves - handling a snake.

Prince Edward watches from the shadows.

Edward was fond of music. John Colon sung to the King 'Cum Serpentibus' (with snakes). In the seventies gogo boys danced naked along the bar tops of New York clubs, and a stripper 'cum serpentibus' performed in the Black Cap pub in Camden Town with a huge python.

Everyone fancied BJ. He arrived in a suit and glasses with his snake Oscar. Kevin fell in love with the snake. BJ insisted on wearing a jock-strap which made us very sad as every part of him was so well developed. Sandy was asked to sew a gold fig-leaf onto the front of BJ's jock-strap but couldn't because it hadn't been laundered. Paul, her assistant, was able to oblige.

Colin MacCabe (my structuralist friend) told me on the corner of Marchmont Street and Rathbone Place: 'The audience is only interested in sex and violence.' So I said to Stephen, who chopped Marlowe up, 'Put sex and violence into every scene.' More of an Elizabethan lay than an Elizabethan play .

And now all the boys are covering up their cocks again, not at all like the good old days of 'Sebastian'.

SEQUENCE 9.

INTERIOR. DESERTED THRONE ROOM. NIGHT.
EDWARD, GAVESTON.

Edward dressed in dazzling gold robes seated on the throne. He stands with open arms as Gaveston walks towards him. Gaveston kneels. He kisses Edward's hand.

GAVESTON   My lord!

EDWARD   Kiss not my hand,
           Embrace me, as I do thee,
           Why shouldst thou kneel?
           Knowest thou not who I am?
           Thy friend, thy self, another Gaveston

Gaveston stands. Takes off coat. Sits on throne.

GAVESTON   And since I went from hence, no soul in hell
           Hath felt more torment than poor Gaveston.

Edward's gold robe establishes him for a moment as 'the King' as in all those camp old costume versions of Elizabethan plays.

The sequins fell off, darling, and sprinkled all over the set and flashed annoyingly in the camera. Patrick spent an age covering them with Fuller's Earth. Ironically I spent an age getting the sword to flash.

There's no food in the Soviet Union according to the papers today. No wonder, they were so busy growing carnations for Brezhnev's funeral.

are the oxygen of life

hetero?
mixed marriages *never* work

SEQUENCE 10.

INTERIOR. BEDROOM. NIGHT.
EDWARD, ISABELLA.

Cold moonlight falls across the bed. Edward lies on his back, dressed in white pyjama trousers; Isabella astride him. She throws her head back, tossing her hair loose, and puts the King's hands to her breasts. The King leaves them there for a moment and then places them at her waist.

She leans forward to kiss the King's mouth. He turns his head away.

She lies on her side and looks at him for a long time. Then she lies on her back, and they both gaze into the dark, holding their breath.

Edward gets out of bed, he pauses for a moment, then leaves. In a corner of the room he hits his head against the wall till it bleeds.

There is the famous tale in which Edward presents the jewels from Isabella's wedding dowry to Piers in front of her at the wedding feast, which so scandalised the Queen's uncles that they left in disgust for Paris.

Isabella was moderately fond of jewels. For the feast of the purification of the Blessed Mary she had 36 pairs of shoes made and the workmen sewed day and night; 5 shillings was paid for candles to keep them busy in the dark.

In the last year of her life living in retirement she spent £1,400 on jewellery.

An unsatisfactory bedroom scene with Tilda and Steven - she thought it might be misogynist, I thought the audience would have some sympathy for her, even if she plays it hard.

We've all met Isabellas, there are hundreds of them in Knightsbridge. Tilda spent a fortune shopping with them for her earings.

Andrew is not playing Gaveston in a way that will endear me to 'Gay Times', only Edward comes out of this well and even he has bloody hands.

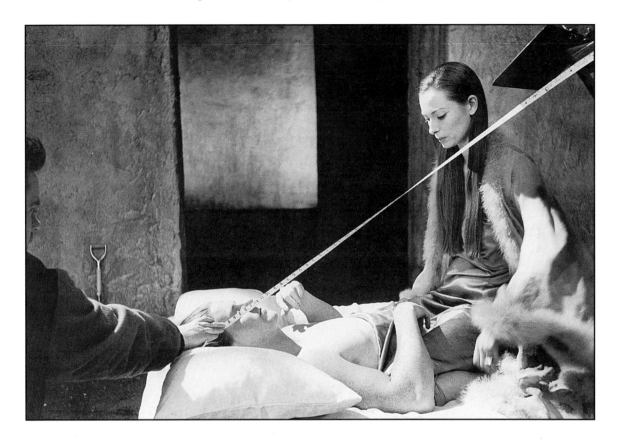

maybe
you're
just
going
through
a straight
phase?

SEQUENCE 11.

INTERIOR. THRONE ROOM. NIGHT.
EDWARD, GAVESTON, PRINCE EDWARD, KENT.

Edward holds a sword. Gaveston kneels before him.

EDWARD   I here create thee Lord High Chamberlain,
(lighthearted) Chief Secretary to the State and Me,
                Earl of Cornwall, King and Lord of Man.
                (He dubs Gaveston with the sword.)

GAVESTON   My lord, these titles far exceed my worth.

EDWARD   Thy worth, sweet friend, is far above my gifts,
                Therefore to equal it receive my heart;
                If for these dignities thou be envied,
                I'll give thee more;
                Want'st thou gold? go to my treasury.

GAVESTON   It shall suffice for me to enjoy your love.
                (They kiss)

EDWARD   Welcome home, my friend.
                (Whispers into Gaveston's ear)

Kent and Prince Edward appear, surprising them from the shadows.

KENT   Brother, the least of these titles may well suffice,
                For one of greater birth than Gaveston.

EDWARD   What - are you moved that Gaveston sits here?
                It is our pleasure - we will have it so.

KENT   My Lord these titles far exceed his worth.

EDWARD   Cease, brother, for I cannot brook these words.

Prince Edward and Gaveston sit on the throne playing with the State
sword like a machine gun.

*Maybe this story should have
been told in a different way with
Piers Gaveston as the wronged
party. After all he had lived with
Edward ten years before the
marriage to Isabella. The
clowning could be a bid for
attention. Not one of the history
books sees it that way, not even
the most sympathetic. Edward's
affections forced by the demands
of Kingship into the heterosexual
marriage bed.*

save | from
queer | straight
children | parents.

SEQUENCE 12.

INTERIOR. BEDROOM. NIGHT.
ISABELLA.

The Queen, distraught with jealousy, hangs over the edge of the bed.

ISABELLA   I love him more
              Than he can Gaveston - would he loved me
              But half so much.
              But half so much
              Were I treble blessed.

Her voice echoes in the empty spaces.

Tilda cut the lines, she probably told me but I didn't take it in. She lay with her hair over the edge of the bed, did nothing. Action. Mesmerised I watched, nothing happened, perhaps she would move, I'd better not say cut, perhaps she was building up to an outburst of genius which I might ruin. So I waited and waited, and Ian looked at me, and I at him, and Tilda didn't move. I said 'cut' quite gingerly, and the longest static take ended on the cutting room floor.

The production department say I'm using too much film. I hardly ever do more than two takes.

Homo *means* Same *means* Equal

SEQUENCE 13.

INTERIOR. THRONE ROOM. NIGHT.
EDWARD, GAVESTON.

Edward and Gaveston. Edward sitting on the throne. Gaveston seated at his feet. The Queen's shouts echo in their laughter.

ISABELLA   But half so much.
(V/O)

Ken, my ghost, pushed me to update the script to the nineties instead of dithering. I insisted that the clothes were not fantasies, a leather jacket from Lewis Leathers, a T-shirt, nothing fancy. Just like Tennessee Williams.

I chose this play solely for its subject. The poetry, like my production values, is of secondary importance.

This sequence read: Edward and Gaveston fuck. The Queen's shouts echoing in their laughter.

I'm not sure why it was changed, but this version came off the disk. Fucking was a problem, I signed minuted notes for the BBC, and the boys found it impossible; they said it was out of place. In the end they had a cuddle. I wanted an act of buggery, like I had performed countless times in private and public, and once for the screen in 'Ostia' for Julian Cole, but the times were not right.

What do you really know

SEQUENCE 14.

INTERIOR. MORTIMER'S BEDROOM. NIGHT. SMALL ROOM. MORTIMER, 2 WILD GIRLS.

Two girls in bed with Mortimer - awakened by the Queen's shouts and the King's lovemaking, Mortimer wakes as well. The girls light a cigarette.

MORTIMER   This Edward is the ruin of the realm.

about Lesbians and Gays?

I was ill today with a temp of 102° so Ken stepped in. The same-sex kiss got a sigh of approval, straight men get off on lesbian sex. The two girls who originally were to do this were warned off by their agent because of my 'reputation'.

Nigel in the leopard skin coat looks very fierce; Jomo Kenyatta.

heterosexuality is cruel & kinky

Neither Edward nor Gaveston were the limp-wristed lisping fags so beloved of the tabloids. Edward swam in winter, hedged and ditched the fields of his house at Langley. Gaveston was the finest horseman of his age.

Andrew (Gaveston) pulled out all the stops, turning himself into a frightful clucking demon. A mesmeric moment.

'If Helen Mirren had played her love scenes like you, the British cinema would have closed its doors even quicker,' I had snapped in the dressing room.

I love Steven's delivery of "Was ever a King so over-ruled as I?"

Cigarettes are banned on the set. This was difficult for some, particularly Ken, the ghost, who chain smokes, and spluttered into the day as we hit the Westway each morning.

It's not much use warning that each cigarette knocks three minutes off your life when a fuck can stop it in its tracks.

SEQUENCE 15.

INTERIOR. THRONEROOM. NIGHT.
EDWARD, GAVESTON, MORTIMER.

Gaveston, naked, is seated on the throne.
Mortimer stands in front of him shaking with anger.

GAVESTON   Were I a King.

MORTIMER   Thou villain.
              Wherefore talks thou of a king,
              That hardly art a gentleman by birth.

Edward appears from behind the throne.

EDWARD   Were he a peasant, being my minion,
              I'd make the proudest of you stoop to him.

MORTIMER   Away I say with hateful Gaveston.

EDWARD   Here Mortimer wear you my crown
              Sit thou in Edward's throne.
              Was ever a King so over-ruled as I?

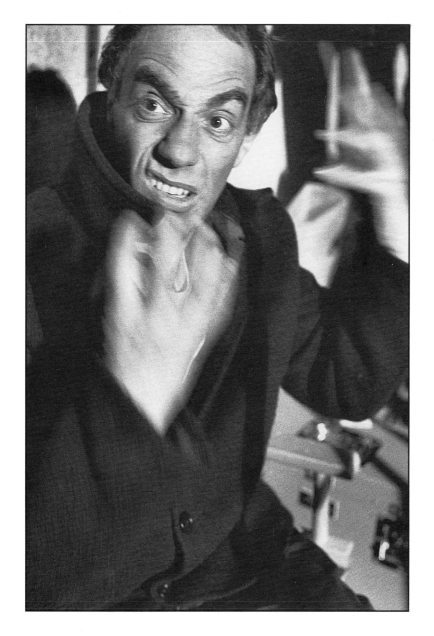

PENETRATE
the Rambo Bimbo
DIVIDE

SEQUENCE 16.

INTERIOR. EMPTY ROOM. DAY.
ISABELLA, MORTIMER, PR. EDWARD, CHORUS OF 12 EARLS.

Mortimer and chorus, who resemble the benches of the House of
Commons, in the shadows discover the weeping queen with Prince
Edward.

MORTIMER   Look where the sister of the King of France,
            Sits wringing of her hands and beats her breast.

CHORUS   The King, I fear, hath ill intreated her.

MORTIMER   Hard is the heart that injures such a saint.

*Chorus materialises like
shadows. Jody switches on a
flashing robot. This is the third
film we've made together. He
was happy not to be in pyjamas
again. Did you wear your
mother's clothes?*

*Mediaeval fag-lore.
Queer hares. "The hare grows a
new anus each year (lucky
for some), hyenas alternate
between male and female each
year." A confusion of lusty
imaginings in the mind of
Clement of Alexandria.*

*"Gay men are unfit to be
ordained as priests."
Ugly Archbishop Carey.*

*"And this is not even the worst,
which is that this outrage is
perpetrated with the utmost
openness." Saint John
Chrysostum. (Where was he?)*

*"Edward in fact delighted
inordinately in the vice of
sodomy." Ralph Higden.*

*I first fucked with a young man
in the basement of 64, Priory
Road. I was 23, it was 1965.*

Open your mind

not your big mouth

SEQUENCE 17.

INTERIOR. BEDROOM. DAY.
EDWARD, GAVESTON, MORTIMER, KENT, CHORUS OF EARLS.

Gaveston, Kent and the King play cards on the bed, surrounded by a pack of beagles. Mortimer and the Earls arrive.

MORTIMER	If you love us, my lord, hate Gaveston.
GAVESTON (Whispered)	That villain Mortimer! I'll be his death.
MORTIMER	These Earls, my lord and I myself. Were sworn to your father at his death That he should ne'er return into the realm.
EDWARD	I will have Gaveston, and you shall know What danger 'tis to stand against your King.
GAVESTON	Well done, Ned!

The hounds are so noisy the chorus has to shout to be heard.

EARL	My lord, why do you thus incense your peers, That naturally would love and honour you.
KENT	Yet dare you brave the King unto his face. Brother, revenge it! And let their heads Preach upon poles, for trespass of their tongues!
CHORUS (Laughter)	Oh, our heads!
MORTIMER	Come, let us leave the brain-sick King

They exit.

"And when the King's son saw him he fell so much in love that he entered into an enduring compact with him." Chronicle of Melsa.

Piers gave nicknames to the Barons; the obese Earl of Lincoln was 'Burstbelly'; Warwick 'The Black Dog of Arden'. The bright young favourite was never short of a bitching remark, nor ever spared it. The Barons retaliated.

"Piers had misled and ill-advised our lord the King, and enticed him to do evil in various and deceitful ways..."

"In what way my brother did you first lose your virginity? By fornication, lawful wedlock, masturbation, or one of those sins that are against nature?" John the Faster.

The film is costing £850,000. Two takes, one for safety. The Beagles' whipper-in is called Bert. He told me if a dog is hurt the others set on it.

The Barons became a chorus. This opens up the play and gives us more womens' parts.

gender is apartheid

INTERIOR. DUNGEON. NIGHT.
EDWARD, LIGHTBORN.

Edward talks to himself feverishly, almost in a trance.
Lightborn strokes the polecat.

EDWARD   (gazing into the pool).

        Two Kings in England cannot reign at once.
        But stay awhile, let me be King till night,
        That I may gaze upon this glittering crown,
        So shall my eyes receive their last content.
        My head the latest honour due to it,
        And jointly both yield up their wished right.
        But hardly can I brook to lose my crown
        And Kingdom without cause.
        But what the heavens appoint I must obey.
        Here take my crown.

Lightborn does not react

EDWARD   Oh, wherefore sits though here?

LIGHTBORN   If you mistrust me, I'll begone my Lord.

EDWARD   No, no for if thou meanst to murder me
           Thou must return again, and therefore stay.

A good morning. Kev (Lightborn) brought Cousin Walter's polecat from Newcastle.

Walter built a fine cage, but the polecat preferred to run 'wild' - under and over the furniture at Phoenix House. It loved the bath, bit me only once on the ankle, sang a lot, and ate quail's eggs and cat food.

After the week spent filming in the dungeon it was quite happy to go home to its friends.

our orientation is not *your* decision

SEQUENCE 19.

INTERIOR. EMPTY ROOM. DAY. STAIRCASE.
MORTIMER, ISABELLA.

Distracted, Isabella walks down the staircase. Mortimer steps forward from the shadows.

MORTIMER   Madam, whither goes your majesty so fast?

The Queen does not stop.

ISABELLA
(Out of
breath)
    Down to the country, gentle Mortimer,
To live in grief and baleful discontent,
For now my Lord the King regards me not,
But dotes upon the love of Gaveston.
He claps his cheeks and hangs about his neck,
Smiles in his face and whispers in his ears,
And when I come he frowns, as if to say,
'Go whither thou wilt seeing I have my Gaveston'.
Is it not queer, that he is thus bewitched?

MORTIMER   That sly inveigling upstart we'll exile
Or lose our lives.

ISABELLA   You know the King is so suspicious
That if he hear I have but talked with you
Mine honour will be called in question.

"That sly upstart (Frenchman)"... We tried to moderate the xenophobia.

For this scene Christopher (the designer) threw up a ramp that was almost impossible to climb. We had an argument about it. He said, well, you saw the model, Derek! Tilda staggered down in a pair of gold high-heels, clutching a little black bag by Hermès that cost £3,900(!) - more than the set. I couldn't walk down it in my sand-shoes. (D)

If a Queen's no good for a 1:1 ramp in stilettos with a Four Grand pocket of crocodile skin clutched to her breast what is she good for? (IR)

The Gangplank, Tilda has to walk down is far too steep - Pearl (continuity) says 'Give her a skateboard.' (G)

Two ladies were in a tea shoppe in Windsor, in walks a slightly windblown lady with Hermès headscarf tied on the chin, tweed suit, corgis at heel, she orders a cake to take out. The ladies look for a while, then have to speak, "Excuse me, we have to tell you that you look just like the Queen." "Good" replies Her Majesty, and leaves. (D)

i wish *my* aunt were a lesbian

SEQUENCE 20.

INTERIOR. BURIAL CHAMBER. NIGHT.
EDWARD, GAVESTON, THE BISHOP OF WINCHESTER,
2 ALTAR BOYS. 4 SOLDIERS ON GUARD.

The body of the King's father lies, dressed in gilded armour.
The Bishop of Winchester blesses the open coffin, supported by two altar boys.

Gaveston enters with Edward.

BISHOP (to Gaveston) Is that wicked Gaveston returned?

Edward hears this and hisses through his teeth.

EDWARD Ay, priest, and lives to be revenged on thee
The only cause of his exile.

BISHOP Gaveston, unless thou be reclaimed
Thou shalt back to France.

GAVESTON And but for reverence of these robes
Thou should'st not plod one foot beyond this place.

EDWARD Ere my sweet Gaveston shall part from me
This isle shall fleet upon the ocean.

The choirboys' names were John-Henry and Thomas. Dudley Sutton played the Bishop.

There was much ado about the way soldiers comport themselves. The armour is gilded with French polish, porphyry base.

Bishop Dudley said 'Shouldn't I be wearing my medals?' An RAF vicar I met was wearing medals he was awarded for the bombing of Dresden. I couldn't see past the charred bodies as we sipped sherry. Marlowe just wanted to drown the fuckers.

Dudley said of 'The Devils' - rape and pillage on every side, and Vanessa Redgrave at the eye of the storm quietly reading a book on Chinese Agrarian reform.

SEQUENCE 21.

INTERIOR. BEDROOM. NIGHT.
EDWARD, GAVESTON.

Gaveston and Edward on bed.

GAVESTON   Gaveston, unless thou be reclaimed
(As Bishop)   Throw off his golden mitre, rend his stole,
                  And in the channel christen him anew.

EDWARD   Ah brother, lay not violent hands on him,
                  For he'll complain unto the See of Rome

GAVESTON   Let him complain to the See of Hell,
(As himself)   I'll be revenged on him for my exile.

Gaveston punches the pillow. Edward flings himself at him.

EDWARD   No, spare his life but seize upon his goods.
(Breathless)   Be thou lord Bishop and receive his rents.
                  I give him thee, use him as thou wilt.

GAVESTON   He shall to prison and there die in bolts.

Today's gossip: Ian has fallen in love all over again with one of the guardsmen in the film.

Ken said it was rumoured that Robert (Mapplethorpe) had picked a victim at the Mineshaft and taken snuff photos. True or not, Robert spent all his life creating rumours about himself. What is true is that Sam Wagstaff, who built one of the greatest photographic collections in the world got into Robert's S&M sculptures and this is how his career started.

QUEENS will not be pawns

Robert believed that like money there was only so much fame in the world and guarded his little patch jealously.

Robert is much like our Piers Gaveston, a sharp hustler. How many friends do you have who have fallen for someone who seems as unattractive as him?

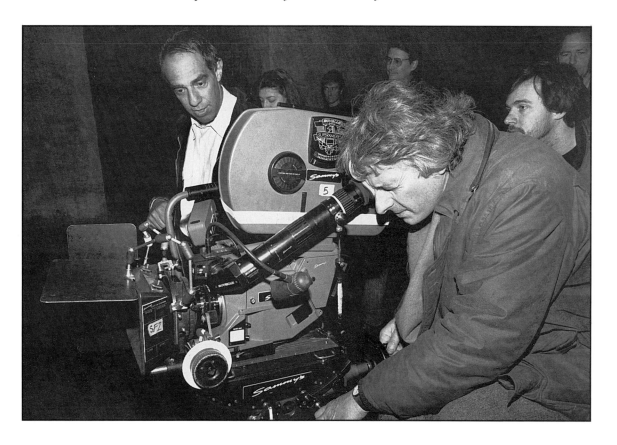

It takes 2 breeders to make queer 1

SEQUENCE 22.

INTERIOR. EMPTY ROOM. MORNING.
GAVESTON, BISHOP, 4 THUGS.

A group of thugs surround the Bishop - his face bruised and bleeding.
He stands vulnerable in his underpants.
The thugs grab hold of him and spin him round.
Gaveston enters. Removes the Bishop's false teeth, crosses him
with them. Pushes him to the ground

GAVESTON   Convey this priest to the Tower.
                A prison may beseem his holiness.

BISHOP   For this offence be thou accursed of God.

Gaveston and Thugs exit.

Thugs = heroes.

Danny Earl, one of the thugs, came up to me in The Presto (my Italian restaurant) and awarded me a medal for service to film. He lives in Brighton, and works at The Alarmist Theatre.

Dudley went further than we expected (!), he dropped his false teeth and his pants. Andrew (Gaveston) looked as if he'd stepped from 'The Krays'. The updating makes this eerie.

I wish *my* father were a lesbian

SEQUENCE 23.

INTERIOR. DAY. STAIRCASE.
ISABELLA, GAVESTON.

Gaveston blocks the Queen's way in the staircase, his jeans and
T-shirt in sharp contrast to her lavish black dress.
His action belligerant, he kisses her contemptuously.

QUEEN　　　　Thou wrongst me Gaveston.
　　　　　　　Ist not enough that thou corruptst my lord,
　　　　　　　And art a bawd to his affections,
　　　　　　　But thou must call mine honour thus in question?

GAVESTON　　I mean not so, your grace must pardon me.
　　　　　　　(Mocking)

QUEEN　　　　Villain, tis thou that robst me of my lord.

GAVESTON　　Madam, tis you who rob me of my lord.

ISABELLA　　　Fair blows the wind for France, blow gentle gale.

Laid low with my stomach and quite exhausted, Ken directed. I'm certain most will see this sequence as an assault on Isabella, though Gaveston's reaction is understandable.

Not all gay men are attractive. I am not going to make this an easy ride. Marlowe didn't.

GOD

WAS A CONFIRMED BACHELOR

SEQUENCE 24.

INTERIOR. BURIAL CHAMBER. NIGHT.
MORTIMER, 4 SOLDIERS ON GUARD. (Chorus of Earls as V/O).

The 4 soldiers guard the King's body. Mortimer stands with them.

EARL (V/O)   First were his sacred garments rent and torn
                Then laid they violent hands on him
                Next himself imprisoned, and his goods aceased.

EARL (V/O)   Tis true the Bishop is in the Tower
                And goods and booty given to Gaveston.

MORTIMER   What will they tyrannise upon the Church?
                Ah, wicked King - accursed Gaveston.
                We may not nor we will not suffer this.

EARL (V/O)   Doth no man take exceptions at the slave?

MORTIMER   All stomach him, but none dare speak a word,
                Thus arm in arm the King and he doth march,
                Nay more, the guard upon his Lordship waits;
                And all the court begins to flatter him.
                This ground which is corrupted with their steps
                Shall be their timeless sepulchre, or mine.

EARL (V/O)   We'll haul him from the bosom of the King
                And at the court gate hang the peasant up
                Who swollen with the venom of ambitious pride
                Will be the ruin of the realm and us.

MORTIMER   The King will lose his crown
                For we have power and courage
                To be revenged at full.

EARL (V/O)   Unless his breast be sword-proof he shall die.

The chorus of Earls build up their parts by adding lines - they all end up on the cutting room floor. (G)

Would have played Tallis, but our budget does not stretch that far - just a funeral bell. But who cares, Simon Fisher Turner is going to turn the noisy brute into a requiem mass.

This was the last day with the earls, much sadness, and many little presents: a pair of ecclesiastical socks from Jill Balcon, and a first edition of James Purdy's '63 Dream Palace' from John Quentin who met him in the fifties. I recommend Purdy for his gripping perverse tales of family terror.

...AND MY FATHER'S FATHER'S FATHER'S FATHER WAS A FILTHY BIGOT

SEQUENCE 25.

INTERIOR. GYM. MORNING.
EDWARD, GAVESTON, MORTIMER, KENT, CHORUS OF
EARLS, GYM INSTRUCTOR, 15 GYM YOUTHS.

Edward and Gaveston work out with the gym youths on the blue
training mats. Mortimer and the Earls enter.

MORTIMER	The idle triumphs, masques, lascivious shows, And prodigal gifts bestowed on Gaveston, Have drawn thy treasure dry, and made thee weak.
CHORUS	Who loves thee but a sort of flatterers?
KENT	Is this the duty you owe your King?
CHORUS	We know our duties, let him know his peers. Why should you love him whom the world hates so?
EDWARD	Because he loves me more than all the world.

*How wonderful to be able to say
these words: 'Because he loves
me more than all the world.' This
should be carved on
Edward's tomb.*

*Everyone thought the gym boys
had worked out too much.*

*Which reminds me, years ago
Mr Belgium came to stay, a
nineteen-year-old hunk. Three
hours in front of the mirror, then
he lay on his stomach to be
fucked, registered not the
slightest bit of pleasure, inert as
a stone; after, he rolled over
heavily and nearly crushed me
to death.*

*The boys were asked to strip off
at Working Title to show off their
bodies. Some were embarrassed,
others had their pants off in a
trice. One of the extras had
pants which proclaimed
'Bear Body'.*

*I've always found gyms
intimidating, my body
gone to seed. I felt intimidated
directing this morning.*

BLEND *the* GENDERS

SEQUENCE 26.

INTERIOR. EMPTY ROOM. DAY.
PRINCE EDWARD. NUDE RUGBY SCRUM.

Prince Edward watches the nude rugby scrum from the shadows.
Sound of clock ticking away.

I have a crazy idea of a naked rugby scrum in August and here it is six months later, looking very much like a 15th century drawing or a hot night in Heaven.

Old friends Philip and Tim put their heads down. Steve Clark Hall (producer) got it going, red and green sides, a Roman chariot race, sex and sport. Boxing and rugby, Australian rules football, all faggot pursuits, locker room stuff.

The boys emerging from the shadows reminded me of ghosts come to haunt me, all my dead friends.

As always life was far more 'advanced' than art. (D)

The rugby scrum (naked) has to be shot. Derek looks at me, and I look at him. How the hell do you direct a rugby scrum? Fortunately Steve Clark Hall (the resident jock) is at hand. He marshals the naked boys into two teams and directs superbly. (G)

Queer as Oscar

INTERIOR. COURTYARD. DAY.
ISABELLA, MORTIMER.

Mortimer and Isabella walk through the castle.

MORTIMER   His wanton humour grieves not me,
                  But this I scorn. That one so basely born,
                  Should by his sovereign's favour grow so pert,

ISABELLA   And riot it with the treasures of the realm,
                  While soldiers mutiny for want of pay,
                  He wears a Lord's revenue on his back,
                  And Midas-like he jets it in the court.

MORTIMER   With base outlandish cullions at his heels,
                  Whose proud fantastic liveries make such show,
                  As if Proteus, god of shapes, appeared,
                  While others walk below, the King and he,
                  From out a window laugh at such as we.

ISABELLA   And flout our train, and jest at our attire,
                  Tis this that makes me impatient.

A small crisis: Nigel and Tilda thought they were doing this scene putting the child to bed. If we had discussed this it completely escaped me.

"Tis this that makes me impatient."
I loved the way these words are spoken by Tilda - they are modern, that much abused word.

Cliff ('I'm not gay') Richard, is in the canteen. 'Thank God he isn't', said Kevin.

7 March 1991, a very Spring-like day. Anthony said he didn't want to see any more of Gaveston's goldfish pout.

hets fear
temptation
not abduction

SEQUENCE 28.

INTERIOR. THE PLOT. NIGHT.
MORTIMER, BISHOP OF YORK, CHORUS OF EARLS.

The conspirators have gathered to sign the form of exile. They sit around a board-room table.

MORTIMER   Here is the form of Gaveston's exile,
                  May it please you to subscribe your names.

CHORUS   Quick, quick, my lord.
                  Give me the paper.
                  I long to write my name.

MORTIMER   The name of Mortimer shall fright the King.
(as he signs)

CHORUS   I long to see him banished hence
                  Unless the King decline from that base peasant.
                  My Lord will you take arms against the King?

MORTIMER   What need I, God himself is up in arms.

Christopher's design for the form of Gaveston's exile has the House of Commons logo.

The green blotters acted as reflectors giving the conspirators a sickish look. Christopher brought in the dispatch box (he is always in the film somewhere). We have been working together now for over twenty years. The table was a copy of the cabinet table.

Should Barbara (who is in the chorus) keep her curlers in as if called out of bed?

Decided not. It might make her look a bit of a joke. We don't want to undermine the opposition in the mind of the audience. If they are dangerous they must appear so. And they are. Read 'Hansard'!

HETEROBNOXIOUS

SEQUENCE 29.

INTERIOR. BEDROOM. MORNING.
EDWARD, GAVESTON, MORTIMER, CHORUS OF EARLS. POET.

Gaveston and Edward seated on golden chairs. A poet reads the opening passages of Dante's 'Divine Comedy'. Mortimer and the Earls enter.

MORTIMER　　　What man of noble birth can brook this sight.

Gaveston sneers.

EARL I
(Woman)　　　See what a look of scorn the peasant casts.

MORTIMER　　　Can Kingly lions fawn on creeping ants?

EARL II
(Man)　　　　Their downfall is at hand.
　　　　　　　Lay hands on that traitor Gaveston.

Edward moves to protect Piers.

EARL I
(Woman)　　　Your grace doth well to place him by your side
　　　　　　　For nowhere else is the new Earl so safe.

Mortimer grabs Gaveston by the hair.

MORTIMER　　　Subscribe as we have done to his exile.

CHORUS　　　　Curse him if he refuse, and then may we
　　　　　　　Depose him and elect another King.

EDWARD　　　　Curse me, depose me, do the worst you can.

Takes the form from Mortimer. Hands it to Gaveston.
Gaveston tears it up.

I like the opening of the 'Divine Comedy', the straight path lost in a dark wood. The byways are the path to the soul, not the highways.

A late snow fell, and we were in our shirt sleeves. So much for spring. We are all exiles here.

HETEROPPRESSIVE

SEQUENCE 30.

INTERIOR. STUDY. DAY.
EDWARD, BISHOP OF YORK.

The bishop, holding the form of banishment, presents it to Edward who sits behind his desk.

BISHOP   Come, come, subscribe.

EDWARD   Ah, none but rude and savage minded men
      Would seek the ruin of my Gaveston.
      You that are nobly born should pity him.

BISHOP   You that are princely born should shake him off.
      For shame subscribe and let Piers Gaveston depart.
      Or I will presently discharge the Lords
      Of duty and allegiance due to thee.
      Are you content to banish him the realm?

EDWARD   I see I must and therefore am content.
      Instead of ink I'll write it with my tears.

Edward signs the form.

BISHOP   Now is my heart at ease.

Steven Waddington was wonderful today. Always go on a hunch, it pays back a hundredfold.

Nigel sent him for the part of Lightborn. He said quite charmingly at our first meeting 'What part should I read for?' I said to him, 'Always go for the top.'

I think he was surprised; he gave me a thrill, he has the red Plantagenet hair, Edward's broad shoulders, fresh looks, and a gentleness that suits a King.

I had always wanted to work with Annie Lennox, so imagine how surprised I was to be asked to do the little film for her Cole Porter song on Leigh Blake's 'Red Hot and Blue'; raising money for AIDS research. And there I was ill in St. Mary's, and the sun shone outside the window and Annie came to see me, so retiring the nurses didn't recognise her... and now here she is singing the song for 'Edward II'.

Whatever is she doing here? Well, if you were King for a day who would you have to sing for you?

Steven said he had fallen in love.

Andrew played this scene with subtlety, I hope you can feel a little pity for him.

A very sweet girl from OutRage came with her girlfriend, I think her name was Becca, they were very happy.

I brought in my yellow hospital pyjamas, Tilda gave me in hospital. Andrew chose to wear the sad green ones.

S E Q U E N C E   3 1 .

INTERIOR. NIGHT.
EDWARD, GAVESTON, ANNIE LENNOX.

The King and Gaveston dance alone in the spotlight.

GAVESTON   My lord, I hear it whispered everywhere
             That I am banished.

EDWARD   Tis true, sweet Gaveston.
             Thou must from hence, or I will be deposed.
             Sweet friend take it patiently
             my love shall never decline.

GAVESTON   Is all my hope turned to this hell of grief?

EDWARD   Rend not my heart with too-piercing words,
             Thou from this land I from myself am banished.

GAVESTON   Seeing I must go, do not renew my sorrow.

EDWARD   Was ever a King so over ruled as I?
             The time is little thou has to stay,
             And therefore give me leave to look my fill.

GAVESTON   Tis something to be pitied of a King.

They kiss.

H E T E R O F F E N S I V E

heterosexuality: an exercise in cultural narcissism

SEQUENCE 32.

INTERIOR. DAY.
GAVESTON, 20 CLERGYMEN.

Gaveston is man-handled between two lines of Clergymen who spit at him.

Never put a man in a uniform.

One of the priests did a number and called for more money, in spite of the fact that they were getting more than the union minimum. Is our budget so tight that we are tight-fisted?

Steve said to the man, "Do you see, I'm smiling, I always smile when I'm shafted."

One of the 'priests' sent me a letter saying how much he had enjoyed the day, they were away by 11:00 and many of them thought the argument for more money well out of order.

The six-day week is gruelling, I'm here at 7:30 am, back home at 8:30 pm.

Ian (who drives me home) cruised a boy all the way through Kensington shouting out of the window of his car - saying 'Haven't I seen you before?'
'Yes.'
'Let's do it again.' I said, and gave him the phone number at Bray. We never heard from him.

homo*équalité*

SEQUENCE 32A.

INTERIOR. DAY.
EDWARD, PRINCE EDWARD, 20 CLERGYMEN.

Edward makes his way through a group of clergymen holding Prince Edward's hand. He bends down to talk to him.

EDWARD How fast they run to banish him I love;
They would not stir were it to do me good.
Why should a King be subject to a priest?
Proud Rome, that hatchest such imperial grooms,
For these thy superstitious taper-lights,
Wherewith thy anti-Christian churches blaze,
I'll fire thy crazed buildings and enforce
The papal towers to kiss the lowly ground;
With slaughtered priests may Tiber's channel swell
And banks raised higher with their sepulchres;
As for the peers that back the clergy thus,
If I be King not one of them shall live.

Pr. EDWARD Why should you love him who the world hates so?

I felt we should change the Rome to Canterbury, or York.

Then decided to leave it as it is, the Roman church has a greater congregation than the Church of England.

Marlowe's atheism is his joy. He would have had no problem putting on a condom.

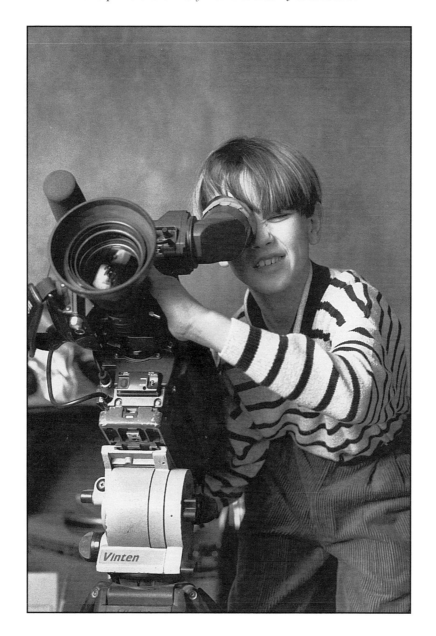

homo *liberté*

SEQUENCE 33.

INTERIOR. ROCK. SUNDOWN.
GAVESTON.

At the edge of the sea Gaveston stands howling. High above him an eagle perched on a rock.

We were to have an eagle, but it laid an egg!

Saturday morning, March 23, our last day. Andrew took a deep breath and plunged into the icy water. When it was over there was a cheer and much sadness. We took the unit photo, and to my surprise and delight I was presented with a Raleigh Chiltern bike for Dungeness. (D)

Tilda played a game with Pat and Dave (props), she asked them for mad props. This morning Pat said 'Thank God Tilda isn't in this scene - or she would have wanted a mermaid's tail.'
David said 'No she wouldn't - she would want to fly in as an albatross.' (G)

homo*sexualité*

SEQUENCE 34.

INTERIOR. DUNGEON. NIGHT.
EDWARD, LIGHTBORN.

Edward sitting by the edge of the pool.

EDWARD   He's gone, and for his absence thus I mourn,
                 Did never sorrow go so near my heart.

The paper today accuses me of making a 'Gay version of Edward II'. They really shouldn't write about things they don't understand. Could Marlowe's poetry describe an ordinary friendship? Has anyone who writes for or reads these papers actually read the play?

Buggery was a good way of slandering someone in the Middle Ages - the Cathar heretics and the Knights Templar, murdered by Isabella's father, Philip. It is just possible that Piers was a victim of this slander but the Vita says 'the King loved him inordinately'.

Other Royal queers? William Rufus, the sons of Henry I who sunk in the the white ship, Henry II, and Richard Coeur de Lion... The present unfortunately has to be misted over. The problem about outing people is that most of them are so unpleasant, one really doesn't want them around; outing should be done from a sense of duty, just like Christian charity.

As for who to out - Labour MPs should be the first target. They're 'meant' to be helping us. Lock the closet key firmly on the Tories.

straights *lie* queers *die*

SEQUENCE 35.

INTERIOR. DAY.
EDWARD, ISABELLA, PRINCE EDWARD, 2 MAIDS, SEAMSTRESS.

Isabella being fitted for a new dress.
The King storms in.

EDWARD	Fawn not on me, French strumpet; get thee gone. Seamstresses exit.
ISABELLA	On whom but on my husband should I fawn?
EDWARD	On Mortimer.
ISABELLA	Thou wrongst me.
EDWARD (Grabs her neck)	Thou art too familiar with that Mortimer, And by thy means is Gaveston exiled. But I would wish thee reconcile the lords, Or thou shall never be reconciled to me.
ISABELLA	Your highness knows it lies not in my power.
EDWARD	Away then. Touch me not.

Edward leaves.

We are all exhausted, Thursday March 14, third week of shooting, midweek blues.

This scene is strong, The last line, "Away then, touch me not", I find frightening.

My niece, Kate Temple, who has worked with Sandy in the costume department, steps in front of the cameras, twelve years after she played Miranda in a glistening dress at Stoneleigh.

Sandy made the costumes for 'Caravaggio'. Working with old friends you have no worries, leave it to them. She also did the present RSC 'Edward', which from the photos looks a little too designed for my taste.

Everyone in the costume department fancies Steven Waddington, but they have a pact that it's all or nothing, all of them in his bed or none at all.

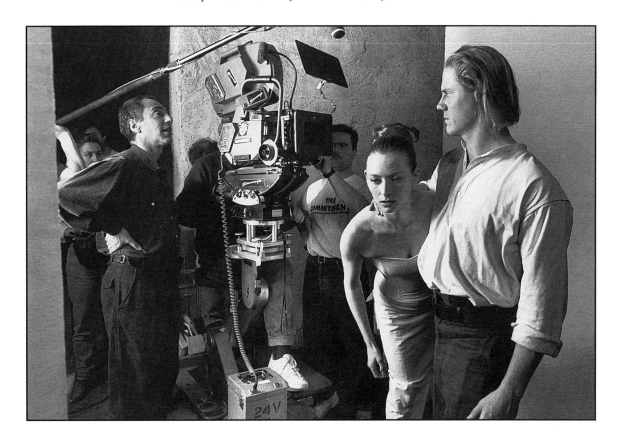

its cool to be queer

SEQUENCE 36.

INTERIOR. DAY.
ISABELLA.

The Queen is alone - slumped down onto her knees.

ISABELLA   Would, when I left sweet France and was embarked,
            That charming Circes, walking on the waves,
            Had changed my shape, or at the marriage day
            The cup of Hymen had been full of poison,
            Or with those arms that twined about my neck,
            I had been stifled, and not lived to see
            The King my lord thus to abandon me.
            I must entreat him, I must speak him fair,
            And be a means to call home Gaveston,
            And yet he'll ever dote on Gaveston,
            And so am I forever miserable.

Home oh home of horrors. (IR)

Tilda's first take took four and a half minutes. George, my editor, looked worried, he said the whole film is stopped in its tracks. I did say rather lamely "We are making a movie... you know 'moving pictures'" to speed things up.

A genuine stock fault came to our rescue, and it now clocks in at two minutes forty five seconds, after removing one and three quarter minutes of pauses.

It's after 8:00 pm, and we've been here since 8:00 am.

to impose
is not
to discover

SEQUENCE 37.

INTERIOR. DUNGEON. NIGHT.
EDWARD, LIGHTBORN.

Edward seated at the workbench. Lightborn sits on the coals to listen to him.

EDWARD   My heart is as an anvil unto sorrow
          Which beats upon it like the Cyclop's hammers,
          And with the noise turns up my giddy brain,
          And makes me frantic for my Gaveston.
          Ah, had some bloodless fury rose from hell
          And with my kingly sceptre struck me dead
          When I was forced to leave my Gaveston.

Ian said both Kev and Tilda had great faces to light. George said Kev's a matinee idol, but tough.

Kev grew his hair for the part and with his Geordie accent and polecat, terrorised me. His great Auntie Bella (94) said to him, "If I was twenty years younger I'd ditch your Uncle Tommy."

on the rim

SEQUENCE 38.

INTERIOR. EMPTY ROOM. DAY.
ISABELLA, MORTIMER. DEAD STAG.

A dead stag is suspended from chains. Drum beats.
Mortimer enters.

MORTIMER   Madam, how fares your grace?

ISABELLA   Ah Mortimer! (fires an arrow)
             Now breaks the King's hate forth,
             And he confesseth that he loves me not.

MORTIMER   Cry quittance Madam, then, and love not him.

ISABELLA   Sweet Mortimer I am enjoined to sue to you for his repeal;
             This wills my lord, and this I must perform,
             Or else be banished from his highness' presence.

MORTIMER   Can this be true, twas good to banish him?
             And is this true, to call him home again?
             Such reasons make white black, and dark night day.

ISABELLA   Do you not wish that Gaveston were dead?

MORTIMER   I would he were.

Round to the back of the sheds to fire bolts into the sandbags. Interesting how many men came by and asked to have a go - implying, Tilda won't need to practise, she stands no chance of hitting anything anyway.

First rehearsal: a miss.

Second for camera: bullseye.

Silence on set.

After that, each shot a palpable hit; I've never been so pleased with three takes in a row in my life. Fuck the scene - I hit the stag! (IR)

Isabella finds herself at the centre of resentment, and isolated. How must Tilda feel about that? (D)

anus

SEQUENCE 39.

INTERIOR. BOARD ROOM. NIGHT.
MORTIMER, ISABELLA, CHORUS OF EARLS.

Mortimer, Isabella and the Chorus sit around the board room table.

MORTIMER   My Lords that I abhor base Gaveston
I hope your honours make no question,
And therefore, though I plead for his repeal,
Tis not for his sake, but for our avail,
Nay for the realms!
Were he here, detested as he is,
How easily might some base slave be suborn'd
To greet his Lordship with a knife.

CHORUS   But how chance this was not done before?

MORTIMER   Because, my Lords, it was not thought upon.

As fast as Patrick cleans the table, the dust resettles. (D)

John, the immaculate couturier, spends days and nights concocting a Charles James ball gown for me with crimson skirts big enough to fill the studio. Derek shoots me from the waist up - ah well. Fashion casualty. (IR)

- the last place the government...

SEQUENCE 40.

INTERIOR. BEDROOM. DAY.
EDWARD, ISABELLA.

Edward hides under the sheets. Isabella enters.

ISABELLA   My gracious lord, I come to bring you news.

She stands at the edge of the bed.
Edward pushes back the bedclothes

EDWARD   That you have parlied with your Mortimer?

ISABELLA   Gaveston, my lord, shall be repealed.

EDWARD   The news is too sweet to be true.

ISABELLA   But will you love me if you find it so?

EDWARD   If it be so, what will not Edward do?

He sits up.

ISABELLA   For Gaveston but not for Isabel.

EDWARD   For thee fair Queen, if thou lovest Gaveston,
I'll hang a golden tongue about thy neck
Seeing thou hast pleaded with so good success.

He kisses her neck.

ISABELLA   No other jewels hang about my neck
Than these my Lord nor let me have more wealth
Than I may fetch from this rich treasury
Oh, how a kiss revives poor Isabel.

EDWARD   Once more receive my hand and let this be
A second marriage twixt thyself and me.

ISABELLA   And may it prove more happy than the first.

...should be poking its nose

STRAIGHT and very *narrow*

SEQUENCE 41.

INTERIOR. DAY.
ISABELLA, KENT, 1 PAGE.

Kent having a massage. Isabella looks on.

KENT   Let him without controlment have his will.
The mightiest Kings have had their minions;
Great Alexander loved Hephaestion,
The conquering Hercules for Hylas wept,
And for Patroclus stern Achilles drooped:
And not Kings only, but the wisest men:
The Roman Tully loved Octavius,
Grave Socrates, wild Alcibiades.
Then let his grace, whose youth is flexible,
And promiseth as much as we can wish,
Freely enjoy that vain light headed Earl,
For riper years will wean him from such toys.

A great outing speech. The classical closet opened. Ian Francis finds many of our extras (soldiers/gym boys) from Covent Garden Sauna. (G.)

The sauna and the steam machines bubbled and wrecked George's sound. Tilda shivered in the cold, the heating is off - it makes such a noise; the jets from Heathrow make a noise; the sparrows in the rafters even more; and the brute splutters, hums and sometimes sings. Andrew, the massage lad from Lees', was very straight, he knew what to do with the oil, his girlfriend was coming round this evening. He was worried he'd not have a close-up.

It's Saturday 23 March, 9:00 in the morning. Tilda decides to break her pearls, everyone is picking up pearls.

Tilda drinks through a straw to protect her make-up - by 9:30 it was finished. (D)

may you

ROT in your hetero heaven

SEQUENCE 42.

INTERIOR. DUNGEON. NIGHT.
EDWARD, LIGHTBORN.

Edward standing in the pool.

EDWARD	The wind is good, I wonder why he stays; I fear me he is wracked upon the sea.
LIGHTBORN	My Lord.
EDWARD	How now, what news, is Gaveston arrived?
LIGHTBORN	Nothing but Gaveston, what means your grace?
EDWARD	They love me not that hate my Gaveston.

The image is the image, and the word, oh don't muck around with that, in the beginning was the word.

Filmed history is always a misinterpretation. The past is the past, as you try to make material out of it, things slip even further away. 'Costume drama' is such a delusion based on a collective amnesia, ignorance and furnishing fabrics. (Lurex for an Oscar). Vulgarity like this started with Olivier's 'Henry V' and deteriorated ever after.

Social realism is as fictitious as the BBC news which has just one man's point of view. Like my film.

Does this answer the question: 'Why are you doing it in modern dress?' Our 'Edward' as closely resembles the past as any 'costume drama' (which is not a great claim).

DEVIATE or *die*

SEQUENCE 43.

INTERIOR. EMPTY ROOM. NIGHT.
EDWARD, GAVESTON, STRING QUARTET.

The String Quartet is playing Mozart. Gaveston enters. The music changes to a tango. Edward embraces Gaveston passionately. They dance.

SEQUENCE 43A.

INTERIOR. EMPTY ROOM. NIGHT.
EDWARD, GAVESTON, STRING QUARTET.

Edward and Gaveston seated on gold chairs.

EDWARD   Thy absence made me droop and pine away
     But now, thy sight is sweeter far
     Than was thy parting hence
     Bitter and irksome to my sobbing heart.

GAVESTON   Sweet lord and King, your speech preventeth mine,
     Yet have I words left to express my joy.
     The shepherd nipt with biting winter's rage,
     Frolics not more to see the painted spring
     Than I do to behold your majesty.

The string quartet played on the lawn at lunch for Annie Lennox and her baby. It was a very sunny day.

Steven and Andrew improvised the dance from 'Some Like It Hot'.

In the end we couldn't afford the tango that they played because every minute would cost us £5,000.

"INTERCOURSE HAS NEVER OCCURRED IN PRIVATE"

SEQUENCE 44.

INTERIOR. NIGHT. CORRIDOR.
ISABELLA, MORTIMER.

MORTIMER   Who's this, the Queen?

ISABELLA   Ay, Mortimer the miserable Queen
            Whose pining heart her inward sighs have blasted
            And body with continual mourning wasted
            These hands are tired with haling of my Lord
            From Gaveston, from wicked Gaveston.
            And all in vain, for when I speak him fair
            He turns away and smiles upon his minion.

Isabella kisses Mortimer.

My ghost, Ken, directed this sequence. I was ill. He directed several scenes and they are some of the best in the film. I don't really need to be there to direct my own films! At St. Mary's I was put on antibiotics for ever as my stomach has been invaded by a bug called campylobacter.

your comfort is our

SEQUENCE 45.

INTERIOR. DAY.
EDWARD, GAVESTON, ISABELLA, MORTIMER, KENT,
PRINCE EDWARD, CHORUS OF EARLS.

A cocktail party. Edward and Gaveston enter.

EDWARD   Will none of you salute my Gaveston?

CHORUS   Salute him? Yes; welcome Lord Chamberlain.

MORTIMER   Welcome is the good Earl of Cornwall.
              Welcome to the King & Lord of Man.

KENT   Brother do you hear them?

EDWARD   Still will these earls and barons use me thus?

GAVESTON   My lord, I cannot brook these injuries.

EDWARD   Return it to their throats; I'll be thy warrant.

GAVESTON   Base leaden Earls that glory in your birth,
              Go sit at home and eat your tenant's beef,
              And come not here to scoff at Gaveston,
              Whose mounting thoughts did never creep so low
              As to bestow a look on such as you.

Mortimer lunges forward and slashes Gaveston.

MORTIMER   Villain thy life.

Isabella runs forward.

ISABELLA   Ah furious Mortimer what hast thou done?

How a space can inhibit you. Something about the way Christopher had placed his columns made me unhappy and we lumped through the day.

Tilda wanted to cut the 'Ah' before 'furious Mortimer'. I asked her to leave that to George the editor. In the event she stood stock still and looked accusingly at Edward? The camera? 'I hate the line.' she said.

The prosthetics annoyed Nigel, he couldn't put the knife in - on the other hand Andrew belted out his lines, he was in his element as class hero.

There was no gossip today. It was such hard going.

SILENCE

anti-queer bigots

SEQUENCE 45.
continued.

Isabella takes the knife from Mortimer's hand.

EDWARD (To Mort.)	Dear shall you aby this riotous deed, Out of my presence! Come not near the court.
MORTIMER (Exiting)	I'll not be barr'd the court for Gaveston, Look to your crown, if you back him thus.
KENT	Mortimer, these words do ill beseem thy years.
EDWARD	Now all of them conspire to cross me thus But if I live, I'll tread upon their heads, That think with high looks thus to tread me down.

Friday March 8, third week of shoot.

Tilda had a special glass that Jill described as a Babycham flute. General bad humour.

Cliff Richard in the dining room looking like an old conker.

We packed up at 7:30.

have small willies

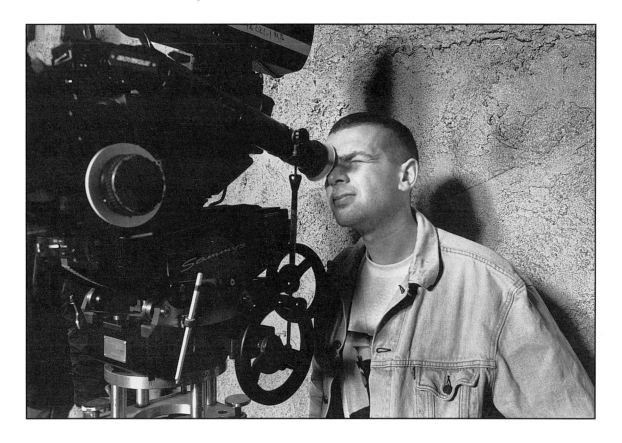

out, proud and livid

SEQUENCE 46.

INTERIOR. DUNGEON. BLAZING FIRELIGHT. NIGHT.
EDWARD, LIGHTBORN.

Edward shouts to the empty echoing dungeon.

EDWARD My swelling heart for very anger breaks;
How oft have I been baited by these peers
And dare not be revenged for their power is great;
Yet shall the crowing of these cockerills
Afright a lion? Edward, unfold your paws
And let their lives blood slake The Furies' hunger;
If I be cruel and grow tyrannous,
Now let them thank themselves and rue too late.

Lightborn is welding.

EDWARD Shall I be haunted thus?

*Eward II (1307-1327) was 23
when he became king. His love
of Gaveston lasted 13 years.*

My temperature is 102°.

HETEROSEXUALITY

SEQUENCE 47.

INTERIOR. BEDROOM. NIGHT.
MORTIMER, 3 WILD GIRLS.

Three wild girls with Mortimer.

MORTIMER   The court is naked, being bereft of those
             That make a King seem glorious to the world,
             Libels are cast against him in the street;
             Ballads and rhymes made of his overthrow.

3 WILD GIRLS   Maids of England, sore may you mourn
(sing)   For your lemons you have lost, at Bannocks borne,
             With a heave and a ho.
             What weeneth the King of England
             So soon to have won Scotland,
             With a rombelow.

We turned this song (put back at the last moment) into a football chant; then cut it in the edit.

Nigel lost his temper as the girls got into the grind with their black leather stilettos. 'Mind what you're doing!' he snapped.

isn't *normal*, it's *just* common

Straights.

S E Q U E N C E 4 8 .

INTERIOR. HOSPITAL. NIGHT.
EDWARD, GAVESTON, SPENCER.

Gaveston sits on the bed. Spencer binds his wounds. Edward sits, watching, holding his hand.

EDWARD   Poor Gaveston, that has no friend but me.

Edward kisses him.

EDWARD   Mortimer is grown so brave
             That to my face he threatens civil wars.

GAVESTON   Why do you not commit him to the Tower?

EDWARD   I dare not, for the people love him well.

GAVESTON   Would Mortimer and Isabella have both caroused
             A bowl of poison to each others health.

He says this whilst looking at Spencer.

EDWARD   Knowest thou him, Gaveston?

GAVESTON   Ay, my lord;
             His name is Spencer.
             For my sake let him wait upon your grace.

Edward puts his finger to Gaveston's lips to stop him speaking.

EDWARD   Spencer, sweet Spencer, I adopt you here,
             And merely of our love we do create thee
             Earl and Lord
             Despite of times, despite of enemies.

SPENCER   My lord. No greater titles happen unto me
             Than to be favour'd by your majesty!

Everyone is shocked to learn that Andrew is 25 and Steven is 23. We thought they were at least 28. Andrew and Steven giggle like schoolboys during the kissing scene. (G)

Funny people but never *very* happy

are *you*
a filthy small-minded

SEQUENCE 49.

INTERIOR. GAME OF SQUASH. MORNING.
EDWARD. KENT.

The set looked its best.
Steven hit Jerome, his best mate,
so hard it made us jump.

The King and his brother, dressed in squash kit - sweating walk through the castle.

KENT   My lord, I see your love to Gaveston
            Will be the ruin of the realm and you,
            For now the wrathful nobles threaten wars,
            And therefore, brother, banish him forever.

EDWARD   Art thou an enemy to my Gaveston?

KENT   Ay, and it grieves me that I favour'd him.

EDWARD   Traitor, be gone! Whine with Mortimer.
(hits Kent, Exits)

KENT   No marvel you scorn the noble peers
            When I your brother am rejected thus.

ANTI-QUEER BIGOT?

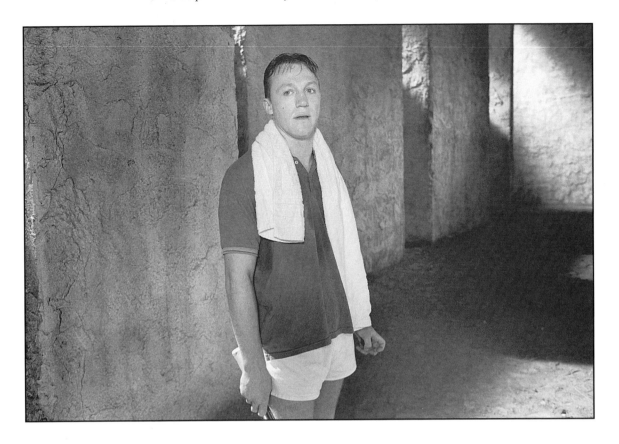

if you must be heterosexual, please *try* to be discreet

SEQUENCE 50.

INTERIOR. FAMILY DINNER. NIGHT.
ISABELLA, MORTIMER, PRINCE EDWARD, KENT.

Having a meal together. Kent enters.

KENT
Of love to this our native land,
I come to join you and leave the King;

ISABELLA
I fear me you are sent of policy,
To undermine us with a show of love.

KENT
Mine honour shall be the hostage of my truth.

MORTIMER
Never was Plantagenet
False of his word.

ISABELLA
Therefore trust we thee.

MORTIMER
Gaveston frolics with the King.
Let us with our followers
Surprise them unawares.

KENT
None be so hardy as to touch the King;
But neither spare you Gaveston nor his friends.

Saturday 16 March.

The spun sugar cake came from Michelle at Maison Bertaux; it's a bit lopsided, as the second chef, who had never made one, did the job - it took three hours and cost £160. The cast are terrorised by it, they are being upstaged and can't see each other.

The sign on Cliff Richard's set has been changed from 'this is a closed set' to 'this is a closet set'.

Today I was told by two journalists, who are both longing to interview me, that their papers the 'Telegraph', and the 'Express', would not carry a story, as my open sexuality would offend their readers.

Bishop Carey's pronouncement that our sexuality cannot be condoned, only forgiven, by his church, adds fuel to the fire. Unnatural, not part of nature; hence the reason for the new book's title 'Modern Nature'.

Get cured -
HOMOPHOBIA is a
social disease

SEQUENCE 51.

INTERIOR. EMPTY ROOM. NIGHT.
EDWARD, GAVESTON, SPENCER.

Gaveston and Spencer with torches. Edward stops them.

EDWARD   Fly, fly, my lord! The earls have got the hold.

GAVESTON   O, stay, my lord! They will not injure you.

EDWARD   I will not trust them, Gaveston; away!

Gaveston exits

EDWARD   Gallop apace, bright Phœbus through the sky,
                And dusky night in rusty iron car,
                Between you both shorten the time I pray,
                That I might see that most desired day,
                When we may meet these traitors in the field.

Cliff Richard is an aging minnow, his evangelical songs work for the enemies of my life. As for anything else, I don't really care.

McKellen's knighthood is more shocking; wining and dining in the erroneous belief that his honour improves our situation. There are many gay men with Tory hearts who believe in this honour. I don't.

It was brave of Ian to come out - but that is all he had to do.

As for the music business that prides itself in its honesty; this is one area they are duplicitous (like Hollywood) - gay sex might damage the till.

Kev leaves for Newcastle to get some sleep. I toss and turn, and my skin is covered with an irritating rash.

SEQUENCE 52.

INTERIOR. NIGHT.
ISABELLA, MORTIMER.

Mortimer standing alone. Isabella enters.

MORTIMER   How comes it that the King and Gaveston is parted?

ISABELLA   That your army, going several ways,
           Might be of lesser force.

MORTIMER   This tattered ensign of my ancestors,
           Which swept the desert shore of that dead sea,
           Whereof we got the name of Mortimer,
           Will I advance.
           And ring aloud the knell of Gaveston.

ISABELLA   Pursue him quickly and he cannot 'scape;
           The King hath left him and his train is small.
           Yet I hope, my sorrows will have end,
           And Gaveston this blessed day be slain.

you're ignorant, arrogant & boring

— we're just a little queer.

The film is coming along. Scene constructed like profiles on a stamp. Tilda looks evil in sick green, clink of ice in her glass, very good.

Happy. (D)

Steve Clark Hall furious at the OutRage boys. I've been sent to Coventry.

Land of hate and bigotry | lesbian and gay rights *now*

SEQUENCE 53.

INTERIOR. HEAVY RAIN. DAY. CORRIDOR.
GAVESTON, 4 YOUTHS.

The injured Gaveston makes his escape with the assistance of four young men.

GAVESTON
(V/O)

Yet lusty lords, I have escaped your handes,
Your threats, your alarms, and your hot pursuits
And though divorced from King Edward's eyes
Yet lieth Pierce of Gaveston unsurprised,
Breathing in hope.

The wind machine roars and sends the flames in the boys' faces.

It's Saturday morning; we cut the scene to make life easier, and to get home by lunch.

I'm so often asked, 'Why don't you make films that are more accessible?' ie: narrative - here's one hiding behind history's jockstrap, but can you imagine an original script on 'Edward II' finding funds? And the cost of narrative makes it prohibitive - essentially narrative is an exercise in censorship because of that.

SEQUENCE 54.

INTERIOR. STUDY. NIGHT.
EDWARD, SPENCER.

Edward very worried at his desk pouring over Ordnance Survey maps with Spencer. The light flickers.

EDWARD   Ah, Spencer, not the riches of my realm
          Can ransom Gaveston! He is mark'd to die!
          I know the malice of Mortimer.

So,
what
do you
think
caused
your
heterosexuality?

On 'The Media Show' A. L. Rowse said Shakespeare was a conservative, Marlowe much more radical. Shakespeare's wilful misinterpretation of the 15th century to bolster Tudor dynastic claims has blighted our past. Crookback Richard will always be that. God save us from genius, though Wittgenstein thought him second rate compared with Michelangelo, or Beethoven (though Wittgenstein could be seen as a mere stutterer).

For the 'Sonnets', though, all Shakespearian historical inaccuracy is forgiven. 'Shall I compare thee to a summer's day?' - I thought of using them as voice-over, then I decided against. 'The Angelic Conversation' is my film of the 'Sonnets'. I have a deep hatred of the Elizabethan past used to castrate our vibrant present.

Sudden thought - lamp should flicker off to end the scene.

You Say
Don't Fuck
We Say
FUCK YOU

S E Q U E N C E   5 5 .

INTERIOR. GALLOWS TREE. GALE. NIGHT.

GAVESTON, MORTIMER, 10 SOLDIERS, 8 POLICE.

Gaveston, covered in mud surrounded by police and soldiers. The Police batter him with their shields. The soldiers stand around.

POLICEMAN   Thou proud disturber of thy country's peace,
                Corrupter of thy King, cause of these broils.

POLICEMEN   Lord Chamberlain.
                Good Earl of Cornwall.
                Lord Governor of Man.

They push him to the ground.

MORTIMER   Monster of men,
              Look for no other fortune, wretch, than death.

GAVESTON   I thank you all, my Lords; then I perceive
              That heading is one, and hanging is the other,
              And death is all.

MORTIMER   Come, let thy shadow parley with King Edward.

Policeman garottes him with his truncheon. The soldiers fire a volley.

Wired up for 'The Media Show'. The blanks in the guns were very loud and dangerous, but Dawn Archibald and her friends insisted they were not blindfolded. My old friend Graham Dowey, who has been in all my films since 'In the Shadow of the Sun' nearly twenty years ago, was a soldier.

We had a discussion as to whether it was 'correct' that all the victims of the firing squad were women - the women didn't really want any male victims. Several sequences have brought up similar discussions.

Ian Francis upset becuase he has to pay the soldiers £25 extra for firing the blanks!

heteros
GOHOMO

SEQUENCE 56.

INTERIOR. FIRELIGHT. NIGHT.
EDWARD, SPENCER.

Edward is numb with grief, Spencer tries to comfort him. They sit
around a campfire.

SPENCER   Were I King Edward, England's sovereign,
             Son to the lovely Eleanor of Spain,
             Great Edward Longshank's issue, would I bear
             These braves, this rage, and suffer uncontrolled
             These Barons to beard me thus in my land,
             In mine own realm? My lord, pardon my speech,
             Did you retain your father's magnanimity,
             Did you regard the honour of your name,
             You would not suffer thus your majesty
             Be counterbuffed of your nobility.
             Strike off their heads and let them preach upon poles;
             No doubt such lessons they will teach the rest
             As by their preachments they will profit much
             And learn obedience to their lawful King.

Edward looks up, exhausted.

EDWARD   Yea gentle Spencer, we have been too mild
             Too kind to them. But now have drawn our sword.

SPENCER   Refer your vengeance
             Upon these barons!
             Let them not unreveng'd murder your friends!

*Peter the boom swinger in the
sound department has a canny
sense of dress. Standing on his box
holding the boom, he looks like a
statue. (D)*

*Derek fancies Peter the boom
swinger and is slightly annoyed to
find him and me talking in the
office at lunch. (G)*

SO ♥ DO ♥ MY ♥ FRIENDS

SEQUENCE 57.

INTERIOR. DUNGEON. NIGHT.
EDWARD, LIGHTBORN.

Lightborn is asleep. Edward grabs hold of a poker.

EDWARD   By earth, the common mother of us all,
                    By heaven, and all the moving orbs thereof,
                    By this right hand, and by my father's sword,
                    And all the honours longing to my crown -
                    I will have heads and lives for him as many
                    As I have manors, castles, towns and towers.
                    Traitorous Mortimer!
                    If I be England's King, in lakes of gore
                    Your headless trunk, your body will I trail
                    That you may drink your fill and quaff in blood
                    You villains that have slain my Gaveston.

He moves the poker across Lightborn's face. Sets it down again.

Edward lies buried in Gloucester Cathedral, in a magnificent alabaster tomb. His body was embalmed; his heart was encased in a silver casket and sent to Isabella. The burial ceremony was magnificent, the body borne through the streets draped in the Royal Leopards of England.

Ralph Higden recounts Edward's death. 'Cum vero ignito inter - Celanda confosus ignominiose peremptus est"

(roughly translated 'with a poker up his arse')

If you go to Gloucester put a flower on Edward's tomb. However, when you do so, remember that he might have got away. A diviner who works for the Police looking for bodies sent me a letter saying that the tomb was empty. So this is why we have a 'happier' ending.

God IS A Black *Jewish* Lesbian

SEQUENCE 58.

INTERIOR. THRONE ROOM. DAY.
EDWARD, PRINCE EDWARD, SPENCER.

The child reads the message from a scrap of paper, he stumbles as he reads.

Pr. EDWARD   The Barons up in arms by me salute
Your highness with long life and happiness,
And bid me say as plainer to your grace,
That if, without effusion of blood,
You will this grief have ease and remedy,
That from your princely person you remove
This Spencer, as a putrifying branch
That deads the royal vine, whose golden leaves,
Empale your princely head, your diadem,
Whose brightness such pernicious upstarts dim,
Say they, and lovingly advise your grace
To cherish virtue and nobility,
And have old senators in high esteem,
And shake off smooth dissembling flatterers.

SPENCER   Traitors! Will they still display their pride?

EDWARD   Rebels, will they appoint their king
His sports, his pleasures, and his company?
Yet, ere thou go, see how I do divorce
Spencer from me.

Edward embraces Spencer

My old friend Peter Docherty comes to the set with one of his students. 'The Late Show' also arrives, and the 'Evening Standard'. I keep an open set as much as possible, there are one or two people here each day.

Simon records the sound of smoke, he's recorded the brute that sings and squeals like a pig, and all the other bumps and grinds of the set - the wind machine, steam machine - all the little bumps and grinds.

JESUS WAS A DRAG QUEEN

SEQUENCE 59.

INTERIOR. TORCHLIGHT. NIGHT.
EDWARD, 30 PEOPLE.

Edward leads the people. The scene resembles the Poll Tax riot.

EDWARD   March with me my friends,
                 Edward this day hath crowned him King anew.

PEOPLE   St George for England and King Edward's right.

Edward stands on a Paganini, a wooden box named after the violinist who was a short man. OutRage are here for the day, sound drums and trumpets!

Peter Tatchell looks after them like a hen with chicks, I rush about as we have never had so many people here in a day, 90, and our resources for looking after them are stretched, and we all want it to be a 'good day'. (D)

The Sisters of Perpetual Indulgence are to make Derek a saint. (G)

OUTRAGE! OUTRAGE!

LESBIANS are *beautiful*

SEQUENCE 60.

INTERIOR. NIGHT. RIOT AND SOUND STUDIO.
ISABELLA.

Isabella harangues the empty room speaking through a microphone.

ISABELLA Misgoverned Kings are cause of all this wrack,
And Edward thou art one among them all,
Whose looseness hath betrayed the land to spoil.
And made the channels overflow with blood
Of thine own people.
And for the open wrongs and injuries
Edward hath done to us, his Queen, and land,
We come in arms to wreck it all with swords;
That England's queen in peace may reposess
Her dignities and honors; and
Remove these flatterers from the King.
That havocks England's wealth and treasury.

I take to wearing my makeup home on the bus. (IR)

Tilda recording her speech, mike stand, spotlight, like 'Evita' - the musical, not the politician.(D)

Derek writes in his gold script: 'Tilda is becoming Isabella!'. (G)

never mind,

SEQUENCE 61.

INTERIOR. NIGHT.
20 POLICE, 30 PEOPLE.

The room is a mêlée of protesters and riot police.
The sounds of protesters amplified. Tear gas.

we
can't
all be
queer

This was fun, invigorating day - preparation for a final shot which I called 'the witnesses'.

Peter Tatchell said that OutRage was a non-violent organisation so the soldiers had to win. I thought we might have beaten one up.

The lads, sixteen of them, blew whistles at Cliff Richard for a minute - quite harmless, but it hit the whole front page of the 'Mirror' next day. This shows how perverse the society is we live in.

The 'Mirror' has 'left-ish' sympathy with a 'right-ish' heart, not that this means much any longer. When it comes to sexual politics left and right never meant much - witness Peter's ejection from the Labour Party and their inability to take our call for equal rights on board. In these matters Britain is so far behind the rest of Europe. It's always a relief to get out of this place, people relate to you so much better on any other street in the world. Hence OutRage beginning a positive campaign here, with 'It's Cool To Be Queer' stickers.

The boys look good and in the end it's all about fucking.

thank GOD FOR lesbians

SEQUENCE 62.

INTERIOR. ABATTOIR. DAY.
EDWARD, SPENCER, CAPTIVE POLICEMAN.

Edward stands victorious over his naked captive - crucified on sides of beef.

EDWARD Vailed is your pride; methinks you hang your head,
But we'll advance, traitor; now tis time
To be avenged on you for all your braves,
And for the murder of our dearest friend,
To whom right well you knew our soul was knit,
Good Pierce of Gaveston, my sweet favourite;
Ah rebel, recreant you made him away.

SPENCER Accursed wretch,
Thou watched the prisoner,
Poor Pierce slain,

CAPTIVE Tyrant, I scorn thy threats and menaces
Tis but temporal that thou canst inflict.
The worst is death, and better die to live,
Than live in infamy under such a King.

Edward stabs him in the stomach.

*'Peace-loving' Archbishop Carey
had SAS marksmen all over
Canterbury Cathedral for his
enthronement.*

*Blood.
Kensington Gore.
Max Factor Massacre.
Claret.*

Morag's SPECIAL MIX.

CONSENTING
GAY
SEX

SEQUENCE 63.

INTERIOR. THRONE ROOM. DAY. BIG ROOM.
EDWARD, KENT, SPENCER.

Edward and Spencer drenched in blood, undress, wash with water
from a bucket.

KENT   A brother? No a butcher of thy friends!
Proud Edward, dost thou banish me thy presence?
But I'll cheer the wronged Queen,
And certify what Edward's looseness is.
Unnatural King, to slaughter noble men
And cherish flatterers!

I have decided to keep bees in Dungeness.

Ian (DP) who keeps them, and Norman (grip) says I should have a WBC hive, it's Edwardian and insulated. Norman won the honey-pot at a show last autumn.

IS NOT A CRIME
CRIME

I AM | THEREFORE
OUT | I AM

SEQUENCE 64.

INTERIOR. DAY. CHRISTMAS TREE.
ISABELLA, PRINCE EDWARD.

ISABELLA   Ah, boy,
              The Lords are cruel, and the King unkind.
              What shall we do?

Pr. EDWARD   Madam please my father well
              I warrant you, I'll win his highness quickly;
              He loves me better than a thousand Spencers.

ISABELLA   Ah boy, thou art deceived at least in this
              To think that we can yet be tuned together
              No, no. We jar too far.

*Tilda's lines were wonderful.
Jody's too much of a mouthful for
him - it was his first time on set
and the first time he'd spoken on
film, poor thing. He was a
little nervous.*

*The Christmas tree and Tilda's
dress fought to upstage
each other. They both turned
out to be gold.*

YOU MADE 100'S OF COMPROMISES TODAY

SEQUENCE 65.

INTERIOR. DUNGEON. NIGHT.
EDWARD. LIGHTBORN.

Edward awake and Lightborn sleeps, a great storm blowing, sound of a
distant battle.

EDWARD   What, was I born to fly and run away?

land of hope and glory*...

INTERIOR. STORM. NIGHT.
ISABELLA, MORTIMER, PRINCE EDWARD, KENT.

Isabella and Mortimer play chess watched by Prince Edward. Kent paces the room distractedly.

KENT   Vile wretch, and why hast thou, of all unkind,
(to himself) Borne arms against thy brother and thy King?

MORTIMER   (Aside to Isabella)
              I like not this relenting mood.

ISABELLA   I rue my lords ill fortune; but, alas,
              Care of my country call'd me to this war!

Kent exits

Pr. EDWARD   I think King Edward will outrun us all.
              Checkmate.

Christopher rushed up a chess set made from peppermills bought in Windsor. I was ill so my ghost Ken took over.

SEQUENCE 67.

INTERIOR. NIGHT.
EDWARD, ISABELLA, MORTIMER, SPENCER, 15 SOLDIERS, 5 PEOPLE.

Edward, surrounded by Mortimer and his soldiers. The King rests his head on Spencer's lap. Spencer gently places his hand on Edward's shoulder.

EDWARD   This life contemplative is heaven.
           On thy lap
           Lay I this head, laden with mickle care.
           Oh might I never open these eyes again,
           Never again lift up this drooping head,
           Oh never more lift up this dying heart.

He closes his eyes.

SPENCER   Look up, my lord, this drowsiness
           Betides no good.

MORTIMER   Here is a litter ready for your grace
           That waits your pleasure; and the day grows old.

EDWARD   A litter hast thou? Lay me in a hearse,
           And to the gates of Hell convey me hence;
           Let Pluto's bells ring out my fatal knell,
           And hags howl for my death at Charon's shore,
           For friends hath Edward none, but him,
           And he must die under a tyrant's sword.

Mortimer helps Edward stand. Soldiers pull Edward to his feet.

SPENCER   Oh day! The last of all my bliss on earth.

*Filmed at a 'Russian angle'.
Seamus said 'it's on the piss'.*

*Meanwhile the problems with
'Modern Nature' keep me up at
night. I can't let the additions
through as I might keel over
before the proof corrections,
something which no-one seems
quite to understand.*

*offer not open to fags and dykes

JOIN THE QUEER NATION

SEQUENCE 68.

INTERIOR. LIGHTNING. NIGHT.
ISABELLA, MORTIMER, PRINCE EDWARD.

Isabella seated at desk. Mortimer and Prince Edward stand beside her.

ISABELLA   Successful battles gives the God of Kings
                  To them that fight in right and fear his wrath.
                  Since then successfully we have prevailed,
                  Thanks be heaven's great architect and you.

MORTIMER   Madam, without offence if I may ask,
                  How will you deal with Edward in his fall?

Pr. EDWARD   Tell me, what Edward do you mean?

MORTIMER   Your Father, I dare not call him King.

Kev's bunch of white amaryllis is brought from Phoenix House, it looks stunning but finds no place on the set. Christopher goes mad about the chair - it has the wrong look. I point out that Isabella's is so expansive that you won't be able to see it. Isabella orders the desk wisely and it centres the sequence.

Kate Temple has baked an excellent cake which is offered around the set. It's raining hard outside, mist shrouds Windsor castle.

Symbolic dust on the desk, backlight shines through ears making them glow red. Everyone in the office smiling again.

SEQUENCE 69.

INTERIOR. DAY. TORTURE ROOM.
MORTIMER, SPENCER.

Mortimer assaults Spencer.

SPENCER   Oh is he gone,
             Is nobel Edward gone,
             Parted from hence, never to see us more?
             Rent sphere of Heaven, and fire forsake thy orb,
             Earth melt to air, gone is my sovereign!
             Gone, gone, alas; never to make return.

Mortimer destroys Spencer.

MORTIMER   Girlboy

open
your
mind

not
your
big
mouth

*Nigel comes up with this great
Jacobean line 'Girlboy'. We add it.*

*'Nigel's takes are always spot-on',
says George (the editor) - 'it's easy
to cut from one of his takes
to another.'*

*The controlled hand-to-hand
violence in the scene is much more
unpleasant than guns.*

YOUR HATRED BECOMES YOU

SEQUENCE 70.

INTERIOR. KING'S BEDROOM. DAY.
ISABELLA, MORTIMER.

Isabella and Mortimer lying on the bed. Mortimer is reading. Isabella has a face-mask on.

ISABELLA   So well hast thou deserve'd, sweet Mortimer,
            As Isabel could live with thee forever.
            Be thou persuaded that I love thee well.

MORTIMER   Fair Isabel now we have our desire
            The proud corrupters of the light-brained King
            Have paid their homage to the lofty gallows
            Edward himself lies in captivity
            And we will rule the realm.

Nigel reads 'Unholy Babylon' - the Life of Saddam. All through this film, war has raged in the Gulf, but there is little time for newspapers or the TV. Our 14th century would be recognised by anyone living in the Middle East. Perhaps it is our 14th century there.

OUTING

SEQUENCE 71.

INTERIOR. DUNGEON. NIGHT.
EDWARD. LIGHTBORN.

Edward sits by the workbench.

EDWARD   Oh water, gentle friend, to cool my thirst
          Oh, Gaveston, it is for thee I am wronged;
          For me both thou and Spencer died,
          And for your sakes a thousand wrongs I'll take.
          If proud Mortimer do wear this crown,
          Heavens turn it to a blaze of quenchless fire;
          Or like the snaky wrath of Tisiphon
          Engulf the temples of his hateful head.
          I see our souls are fleeted hence.
          We are deprived the sunshine of our life.

*In our film all the OutRage boys
and girls are inheritors of
Edward's story.*

it's the least we can do.

DON'T CRY. MAYBE YOU'RE

JUST GOING THROUGH A STRAIGHT PHASE.

SEQUENCE 72.

INTERIOR. KING'S BEDROOM. NIGHT.
ISABELLA, LIGHTBORN.

Lightborn kneels in front of Isabella.

LIGHTBORN   Tis not the first time I have killed a man;
                       I learned in Naples how to poison flowers,
                       To strangle with a lawn thrust through the throat,
                       To pierce the wind-pipe with a needle's point,
                       Or whilst one is asleep, to take a quill
                       And blow a little powder in his ears
                       Or open his mouth and pour quicksilver down.

Isabella kisses him on the mouth.

LIGHTBORN   But yet I have a braver way than these.

She kisses him again.

LIGHTBORN   I, I, and none shall know which way he died.

ISABELLA   I care not how it is so it be not spied.
                  Commend me humbly to his majesty,
                  And tell him that I labour all in vain
                  To ease his grief and work his liberty.

She cuts a lock of her hair.

ISABELLA   And bear him this, as witness of my love.

ISABELLA   (Decisively)
                  He shall be murdered when the deed is done.

Kev, delivering his lines in Geordie, changes the words to fit. Ears became 'lugs', mouth becomes 'gob'. Tilda is quiet, conspiratorial, dream-like. Ian said afterwards 'She's a cross between Joan Crawford and Christine Keeler.'

It's strange how the echo of period in her costumes had everyone remembering movie history. Someone else said Hepburn.

Tilda said as long as they don't all agree on the reference - she's happy.

LAWS MAKE NATURE

INTERIOR. THRONE ROOM. DAY.
ISABELLA, MORTIMER.

Mortimer and Isabella, outrageously bejewelled and made-up, sit on the throne, delirious and drunk with power.

MORTIMER   I seal, I cancel, I do what I will.
                  Feared am I more than loved, let me be feared,
                  And when I frown, make all the court look pale.
                  I am protector now.
                  Now all is sure, the Queen and Mortimer
                  Shall rule the realm, the King; and none rule us.
                  Mine enemies will I plague, my friends advance,
                  And what I list command.

ISABELLA   Sweet Mortimer, the life of Isabel,
                  Be persuaded that I love thee well.

I hope this scene makes you laugh as much as it did us filming it. Tilda's hand swivels like a radar arm at an airport - through 180°. Nigel seemed very happy as well.

STOP
the STRAIGHT WAR
AGAINST
QUEER LOVE

SEQUENCE 74.

INTERIOR. EMPTY ROOM. DAY.
ISABELLA, MORTIMER, KENT, PRINCE EDWARD.

*Lights have their own language:
save the brute, trim the brute, tilt
the willy, kill the blonde, put
a red up, make it Chinese.*

The official photographer is photographing Isabella, Mortimer.
Kent and Prince Edward.

Pr. EDWARD	Let him be King; I am too young to reign.
ISABELLA	Be content, seeing it is your father's pleasure.
Pr. EDWARD	Let me see the King first, then I will.
KENT	Ay, do, sweet nephew.
ISABELLA	Brother, you know it is impossible.
Pr. EDWARD	Why, is he dead?
ISABELLA	No, God forbid!
KENT	I would those words proceeded from your heart!
MORTIMER	(To Prince Edward) My Lord, he hath betrayed the King his brother, And therefore trust him not.
ISABELLA	Come, son, and go with this gentle lord and me.
Pr. EDWARD	With you I will, but not with Mortimer.
MORTIMER	Why, youngling Then I will carry thee by force away.
Pr. EDWARD	Help, Uncle Kent! Mortimer will wrong me.
KENT (Aside)	O, miserable is that common-weal, Where Lords keep courts, and Kings are locked in prison.

SEQUENCE 75.

INTERIOR. DUNGEON. NIGHT.

EDWARD, LIGHTBORN.

Edward stands at the workbench

EDWARD   My daily diet is heart-breaking sobs
            That almost rents the closet of my heart.

Lightborn enters

LIGHTBORN   The Queen sent me to see how you were used,
            For she relents at this your misery.

EDWARD   Tell Isabel, whose eyes have turned to steel,
            Will sooner sparkle fire than shed a tear,
            This dungeon where they keep me is the sink
            Wherein the filth of all the castle falls.
            And there in mire and puddle have I stood
            This ten days space, and lest that I should sleep,
            One plays continually upon a drum;
            They give me bread and water being a King,
            So that for want of sleep and sustenance
            My mind's distempered and my body's numbed,
            And whether I have limbs or no I know not;
            Oh would my blood dropped out my every vein
            As doth this water from these tattered robes.

LIGHTBORN   Oh speak no more, my lord, this breaks my heart!

Edward reaches out for Lightborn's hand. Their fingers touch.

LIGHTBORN   Lie down and rest.

EDWARD   If gentle words might comfort me,
            Thy speeches long ago had eased my sorrows,
            For kind and loving thou hast always been.
            The griefs of private men are soon allayed
            But not of Kings; the forest deer being struck
            Runs to an herb that closeth up the wound
            But when the imperial lion's flesh is gored
            He rends and tears it with his wrathful paw
            And highly scorning that the lowly earth
            Should drink his blood, mounts up into the air;
            And so it fares with me.

LIGHTBORN   Be patient cease to lament
            Imagine this dark prison were your court.

nuclear

family

free

ZONE

REAL MEN
TAKE IT UP THE
arse

SEQUENCE 76.

INTERIOR. DAY.
ISABELLA, MORTIMER, KENT, PRINCE EDWARD.

Kent handcuffed to a chair

MORTIMER	Did you attempt his rescue?
KENT	He is our King.

Mortimer punches him in the stomach.

Pr. EDWARD	He is my uncle.
MORTIMER	He is your enemy.
KENT	Art thou King? Must I die at thy command?
	Either my brother or his son is King.
	And none of both them thirst for my blood.

(He is killed by Isabella biting him on the neck)

Pr. EDWARD	What safety may I look for?
ISABELLA	(wiping the blood from her face)
	Fear not, sweet boy;
	Had your uncle lived, he would have sought thy death.
	He is a traitor think not on him. Come.

I took a swig of blood, just too much, camera turns, action. I jerked my head and began suddenly to choke - panic - should I keep going - will anyone notice - no-one has, stumble on, can't breathe (there is a film in my head - after my funeral Derek suggests they use the film of me choking ANYWAY: "It's what she would have wanted.") Camera still running, I give up and admit "I'm about to die myself..." (IR)

Lo, (Tilda's and Derek's agent) visits the set. Tilda is murdering Kent. I say she will be inundated with parts for horror movies. Derek roars with laughter and says she should have been in 'The Addams Family' - Lo looks worried. (G)

9 OUT OF 10 BABIES *are duds*

SEQUENCE 77.

INTERIOR. DUNGEON. NIGHT.
EDWARD, LIGHTBORN.

Edward lies on the coal.

EDWARD   Something still buzzeth in my ears,
          And tells me if I sleep I never wake.

He pauses and looks at Lightborn who enters carrying a poker.

EDWARD   (Very calmly)
          I know thou com'st to murder me.

LIGHTBORN What means your highness to mistrust us?

EDWARD   Ah, pardon me grief makes me lunatic.
          Know that I am a King - oh at that name
          I feel a hell of grief! Where is my crown?
          Gone, gone, and do I remain alive?

LIGHTBORN These hands were never stained with innocent blood.
          Nor shall they now be tainted with a King's.

EDWARD   Farewell; I know the next news that you bring
          Will be my death; and welcome shall it be.
          To wretched men death is Felicity.
          All places are alike,
          And every earth is fit for burial.

We've adopted the conspiracy theory for the end of the film. Manuel Fieschi, writing to Edward III, told him that his father had escaped from Berkeley Castle, to Corfe, and from there to Avignon, where he was received by Pope Urban XXII, and from there he made his way to North Italy, to become a hermit living a life of prayer.

Too ill to film today. (D)

WE
COMPLICATE
YOU

SEQUENCE 78.

INTERIOR. DUNGEON. THE MURDER. NIGHT.
EDWARD, LIGHTBORN. 4 JAILORS.

The murder seen as a premonition. Lightborn destroys Edward
with the red hot poker.

*Woke up and thought - Oh the
poker scene today, what will Derek
do? How Michael Winner will he
be? Derek didn't show - was
not well.*

*I didn't know what to do, thought I
had better take five deep breaths
and pretend I knew what
to do. Steven had lost his voice so
the screams for five miles around
were lost to sync. Ian made the
scene as red/hellish as possible and
Kevin acted with the precision of a
surgeon. We didn't film Steven's
bum - what a pity. (G)*

Rabbits BREED LIKE *straights*

SEQUENCE 79.

INTERIOR. DUNGEON. NIGHT.
EDWARD, LIGHTBORN.

EDWARD   These looks of thine can harbour nought but death,
        I see my tragedy written on thy brows.
        Yet stay a while; forbear thy bloody hand
        And let me see the stroke before it comes.

Suddenly and unexpectedly Lightborn takes the poker and throws it into the water. He comes over to Edward and kneels and kisses him.

EDWARD   Continue ever, thou celestial sun;
        Let never silent night possess this clime.
        Stand still you watches of the element,
        All times and seasons, rest you at a stay
        That Edward may be still fair England's King.

Then this scene, the surprise, the 'happy ending'. Derek says Marlowe is lucky to have us: we have rescued the play! (G)

After we had the scene in the can, Liam, the stills photographer, wanted some shots. Kevin and Steven had to kiss for five minutes; at the end of it Kevin felt faint but looked happy enough.

BOYS MUST *NOT* BE BOYS

SEQUENCE 80.

INTERIOR. THE CAGE. NIGHT.
MORTIMER, ISABELLA, PRINCE EDWARD.

Prince Edward dances on top of the cage. Mortimer and Isabella are in the cage covered in white flour. Prince Edward watches them.

MORTIMER   Base fortune, now I see, that in thy wheel,
                There is a point to which when men aspire,
                They tumble headlong down; that point I touched
                And seeing there was no place to mount up higher
                Why should I grieve at my declining fall?

Prince Edward watches them.

Jody in make-up and his mother's silver earings listening to 'The Dance of the Sugar Plum Fairy' on his Walkman. (Did you know that Tchaikovsky was forced to commit suicide?)

Should Jody wear his mother's clothes? Half the crew admit to at least clod-hopping around in their mother's shoes as children wearing jewellery. (G)

Mortimer was executed in the Tower. Isabella was banished from the court on a pension of £3,000 a year; she lived in Castle Rising in Norfolk and died in 1358, buried in the habit of a poor Clare. Edward III had lots of children. If this story seems confusing consult Para. 16 (now deleted) or a social worker.

BABIES:

WITNESSES

FOR THE

PROSECUTION

SEQUENCE 81.

INTERIOR. THRONE ROOM. DAY.
PRINCE EDWARD.

Prince Edward is seated on throne wearing gold robes, crown and holding an orb.

Pr. EDWARD   But what are Kings, when regiment is gone,
But perfect shadows in a sunshine day?
I know not, but of this I am assured,
That death ends all, and I can die but once.
Come death, and with thy fingers close my eyes,
Or if I live let me forget myself.

This would have made a great ending, but did not work, unfortunately. It has always seemed incomprehensible to me that anyone should worry too much about their children growing up gay. There are much more important things to worry about after all.

SEQUENCE 82.

INTERIOR. THRONE ROOM. DAY.
EDWARD.

Edward stands alone at the top of the stone ramp.

EDWARD   But what are Kings, when regiment is gone,
                But perfect shadows in a sunshine day?
                I know not, but of this I am assured,
                That death ends all, and I can die but once.
                Come death, and with thy fingers close my eyes,
                Or if I live let me forget myself.

He turns away - raises his arms to the heavens.

We are having a good time here.
(8 June 1991)

FINIS

HETEROPHOBIA

liberates

HOMOSEXISM

empowers